SOTHIS PRESS

Sothis Press aims to completely reimagine the public domain book with an emphasis on universal access to captivatingly designed print editions. We believe that technology will enable every single book ever published to be perpetually accessible in beautiful print form. Sothis is beauty in ubiquity.

www.sothis.press
1 Waterhouse Square, London, ECIN 2ST

The Wu Shih Shan Trial

Report of the Case of Chow Chang Kung, Lin King Ching, Loo King Fah, Sat Keok Min, Directors of the Taou Shan Kwan Temple, at Wu Shih Shan, Foochow, Versus Rev. John R. Wolfe, of the Church of England Missionary Society

Fu-Chou Shih

SOTHIS PRESS

ISBN 978-1-0368-0733-7

The Wu Shih Shan Trial
is in the public domain.

This edition is published by
Sothis Press The company
is registered in England and Wales.
The Company Number is 14900389.

THE WU SHIH SHAN TRIAL.

REPORT

OF THE CASE OF

CHOW CHANG KUNG, LIN KING CHING, LOO KING FAH, SAT KEOK MIN,

DIRECTORS OF THE TAOU SHAN KWAN TEMPLE, AT WU SHIH SHAN, FOOCHOW,

VERSUS

REV. JOHN R. WOLFE,

OF THE CHURCH OF ENGLAND MISSIONARY SOCIETY.

(REPRINTED FROM THE "HONGKONG DAILY PRESS").

HONGKONG:
PRINTED AT THE "DAILY PRESS" OFFICE,
WYNDHAM STREET.

1879.

922 C

THE WU SHIH SHAN CASE.

IN H.B.M. SUPREME COURT FOR CHINA.

April 30th, 1879.

BEFORE HIS HONOUR CHIEF JUSTICE FRENCH, SITTING AT FOOCHOW.

CHOW CHANG KUNG AND OTHERS v. THE REV. JOHN R. WOLFE.

This was an action brought by the Directors of the Taou Shau Kwan Temple, Wu Shih Shan, Foochow, against the Rev. J. R. Wolfe, of the English Church Missionary Society, to have the rights of the parties in relation to certain land occupied by the defendant defined. Mr. T. C. Hayllar, Q.C., appeared for the plaintiffs, and Mr. N. J. Hannen for the defendant.

The court room at the Consulate being too small to accommodate the number of people who were expected to attend a large room in a vacant house was engaged for the occasion, and during the greater part of the day it was crowded, both Europeans and Chinese evincing great interest in the case. Amongst those present in Court were Sir Thomas Wade, Mr. Consul Sinclair, Their Excellencies Fang Taotai, Shing Taotai, and several other mandarins, who all appeared in their official robes, with a number of ladies.

Before proceedings were commenced Mr. Hayllar was, on the motion of Mr. Hannen, formally admitted to the bar of the Supreme Court for China.

The pleadings in the case were as follows:—

IN HER BRITANNIC MAJESTY'S COURT AT FOOCHOW.

The 2nd of April, 1879.

BETWEEN

CHOW CHANG KUNG, LIN KING CHING, LOO KING FAH, and SAT KEOK MIN, Directors of the Taou Shan Kwan Temple, situate at Wu Shih Shan, in the City of Foochow, in the Empire of China, Plaintiffs;

and

The Reverend JOHN R. WOLFE, a British subject and a clerk in Holy Orders, residing at Foochow aforesaid, who is also sued on behalf of the English Church Missionary Society, Defendant.

To CHARLES A. SINCLAIR, Esquire, Her Britannic Majesty's Consul at Foochow.

The re-amended Petition of CHOW CHANG KUNG, LIN KIN CHING, LOO KI G FAH, and SAT KEOK MIN, the above-named plaintiffs, shows as follows:—

1.—The Taou Shan Kwan Temple situate at Wu Shih Shan in the city of Foochow together with the buildings and lands belonging thereto are the property of the city of Foochow. The direction and management of the said Temple lands and premises and the control and expenditure of the funds belonging thereto are vested in directors duly appointed. The plaintiffs CHOW CHANG KUNG, LIN KING CHANG, LOO KING FAH, and SAT KEOK MIN are four of the said directors and sue for themselves and the other directors.

2.—The Defendant is a subject of Her Britannic Majesty and a clerk in Holy Orders residing at Foochow and performing there the duties of a Missionary of the English Church Missionary Society of which said Society he is the responsible head at Foochow.

3.—In all cases where licence to build in the locality of Wu Shih Shan has been applied for by foreigners great care has been exercised in providing regulations touching the height and nature of the structure to be erected and the boundaries of the land to be built upon.

4.—In or about the Christian year 1850 the representatives at Foochow of the English Church Missionary Society first obtained a lease of premises at Wu Shih Shan. The representatives were the Reverend ... WELTON and the Reverend ... JACKSON, and by an agreement of rent in the Chinese language bearing date the 18th December 1850 and purporting to be made by and between the said WELTON and JACKSON, SHING the Haukwan District Magistrate, CHARLES A. SINCLAIR the Interpreter to the British Consulate at Foochow, and a certain Taouist Priest named LIN YUNG MOW, it was, after reciting that the said Missionaries were in want of houses for their residence, agreed that the said Missionaries thereby rented from the said Taouist Priest two houses situated respectively at the back and front of the left hand of the Taou Shan Kwan at Wu Shih Shan which were specified as follows:—One house with five rooms in a row broadwise to which was attached an outhouse and an open yard at back and front. One house with four rooms in a row broadwise at the back to which was attached an outhouse having an upper storey of two rooms and a lower storey of one room and an open yard. It was also thereby agreed that the rent of the above houses should be $100 per annum, and that rent for three months should be paid in advance, that the payments should be made according to the English Calendar, that the said Taouist Priest should not interfere with or obstruct any works that might be going on or repairs that might be made inside the houses, which were to be done at the expense of the lessees; that it should be at the option of the lessees to continue the hiring of the said houses and that the said Taouist Priest should not be at liberty to let them to other persons. The said document bears the British Consular Seal and that of the Haukwan District Magistrate.

5.—The above-mentioned two houses were Chinese built and were erected on land belonging to and formed part of the out-buildings of the Taou Shan Kwan Temple. Having entered into possession thereof under the said agreement of rent the said lessees did subsequently remove the said two houses and erect in their stead two structures of foreign design occupying sites considerably larger than those of the original buildings. One of these new buildings the said lessees used as a dwelling house, while the other they employed as a school house for girls.

6.—In the Christian year 1855 the said English Church Missionary Society being then represented at Foochow by the Reverend . . . FEARNLEY and the said Mr. WELTON, by an agreement of rent in the Chinese language made by and between a Taouist Priest of the said temple named CHUNG YUEN CHING and the said Messieurs FEARNLEY and WELTON, but without the consent or knowledge of any one authorized in that behalf, agreed to rent and the said Priest agreed to let to the said two Missionaries a row of four rooms going straight in situated on the right hand side of the said Taou Shan Kwan Temple. It was thereby agreed that the annual rent thereof should be $20 payable quarterly and that the said tenants should pay rent before they could enjoy the occupation of the said premises. It was also agreed that no rent would be allowed to fall into arrear and that should it fall into arrear the said CHUN YUEN CHING might resume and let the property to other persons and that if rent was properly paid the said property might not be let to any one else. The said document was not recorded at the British Consulate, nor did it bear the said Consular seal, nor that of the Haukwan District Magistrate.

7.—The said row of four rooms comprised three dwelling rooms and one servant's room, and were of the same description as the surrounding native houses. The said Missionaries having entered into possession of the said rooms did alter and extend the said rooms by adding an upper storey and other rooms below.

8.—A certain Reverend GEORGE SMITH, a Missionary of the said English Church Missionary Society, did, at some time unknown to the plaintiffs, but previous to the Christian year 1867, without any authority, verbally rent from a certain Priest of the said Temple, a small piece of land the property of the said Temple, and lying contiguous thereto. The situation and boundaries of the said piece of land have never been ascertained or agreed upon, and up to the present time are in dispute.

9.—In or about the Christian year 1862 or 1863 the defendant arrived in Foochow and from or soon after the time of his arrival he has actively interfered in, or has had the management of the affairs of the said English Church Missionary Society so far as they relate to the property at Wu Shih Shan which forms the subject of the present suit, and he has made frequent attempts to get a perpetual lease thereof.

10.—In or about the 12th moon of the 4th year of Tung Chi (1865) the defendant obtained from the said Taoist Priest, CHUN YUEN CHING, without the knowledge or authority of the Proprietors or Directors of the said Temple, a document purporting to convey to the said Defendant for the consideration of $800 paid by him to the said Priest, a perpetual lease of the hereinbefore mentioned lands, buildings, and premises. Upon this fact coming to the knowledge of the said Directors they caused the said lease to be cancelled.

11.—Again in the 5th moon of the 5th year of Tung Chi (1866) the Defendant without the authority or knowledge of the Proprietors or Directors of the said Temple obtained from the said Taouist Priest, CHUN YUEN CHING, another document purporting to convey to the Defendant for the consideration of $500 paid by him to the said Priest, a perpetual lease of the hereinbefore mentioned lands buildings and premises situated on the right and left hand sides of the said Taou han Kwan Temple. The said document was forwarded to the local Chinese Authorities through the British Consulate with a view to its being registered. Upon these facts being brought to the knowledge of the said Directors of the said Temple the said Priest was handed over to the local Chinese Authorities for examination and punishment and he was duly punished. An inquiry into the matter was also held by the British Consul, Mr. CARROLL, who formally decided that as the premises could not be leased for a perpetual term on account of their being property maintained by subscription by the gentry and people, the property should be annually hired as before, and that the said last mentioned agreement should be withdrawn and returned to the defendant. This was accordingly done.

12.—This decision notwithstanding, the defendant did again on the 4th day of the 7th moon of the 5th year of Tung Chi (August 13th, 1866) obtain from the said CHUN YUEN CHING a document in the Chinese language, translation whereof is as follows, that is to say:—

A note of money borrowed made by CHUN YUEN CHING a Taouist Priest of the Taou Shan Kwan, who having now borrowed of Mr. WOLFE a British missionary $500 personally agrees to pay interest upon the amount at the rate of two and two per cent. per mensem that is $11 per month which is to be deducted quarterly from the amount of rent of $33 payable quarterly by Mr. WOLFE. The rent will not be paid till the loan is refunded and before the repayment of the said loan neither the Taouist Priest himself nor any of the other Priests at the Temple shall call to collect the rent. None of the missionaries whoever they be shall after the return of Mr. WOLFE to England be called upon to pay rent. If the Priest wish to collect the rent it is proper that the loan should be refunded to the British missionary and then the Priest may again collect the rent quarterly. Fearing words of mouth will not afford evidence this note of money borrowed is therefore drawn up to serve as proof.

Witness
(Signed) SIT MING YUNG. A Taouist Priest.
(Signed) CHUN YUEN CHING,
maker of the above note.
Tung Chi 5th year, 7th moon, 4th day.
August 13th, 1866.

13.—On the 10th day of the 7th moon of the 4th year of Tung Chi (1 65) an official communication was received by the Prefect of Foochow from the then British Consul, forwarding a petition from the defendant which represented that as violent beggars repaired to the outside of his house to lodge for the night, and bad odours were caused by the large number of dead bodies of infants always thrown at his door, he desired to have added to his house some spare ground measuring from 4 to 5 changs in length and from 2 to 3 changs in breadth in order that he might put up an enclosing wall with a view of excluding these nuisances and prayed that for the above purpose he, the defendant, might be allowed to erect an enclosing wall on the spare ground just outside his door. After an inspection of the *locus in quo* on the part of the local authorities the prayer of the said petition was granted and the desired wall was erected by the defendant.

14.—In or about the 8th moon of the 5th year of Tung Chi (corresponding to the month of September, 1866) an Agreement of Rent in the Chinese language was made and entered into between the defendant and others of the said English Church Missionary Society and the gentry of the City of Foochow and the Directors of the Taou Shan Kwan Temple translation whereof is as follows:

An agreement of Rent made by missionary JOHN WOLFE and others of the Church Mission of England. As they wish to rent a piece of Government ground close by the 'Wun Chang Kung' temple of the 'Taou Shan Kwan' temple in the district of 'Hau Kwan' for building purposes, and as the local authorities have been communicated with by Consul 'Kah' (CARROLL) and at his request the gentry and directors of the said place have been invited to go with them and make a clear inspection of the dimensions of the said piece of land it is found that the ground on the East side thereof abuts on the boundary of the house of the 'Chea' family, on the West side thereof on that of the house of the "Chang" family, on the south side thereof on that of the 'Lee Choe Kung' temple, and on the north side thereof on the hill path: measuring 15 kungs (5 to 6 feet) in breadth, and 18 kungs in length. The houses to be built thereon will be of the same description as those in the neighbourhood—not detrimental to the position of the neighbouring native houses. The ground is rented through CHOW FUNG YUEN and other gentry and directors of the 'Wun Chang Kung' temple duly appointed at a public meeting, for fifteen foreign dollars of full weight per annum, which rent is to be handed over to the British Consul annually in advance without default, for transmission to 'CHOW' and the other gentry, to be spent in aid of the cause of 'Respect for written papers' in 'Wun Chang Kung." The tenants shall from this date build houses within the boundary as above described, without the least encroachment, and the houses so built shall not be higher than the neighbouring native houses or to the detriment of their positions. As this is Government ground it shall on no account be sublet to other persons for building houses thereon, it is leased for a term of twenty years; at the expiration of the said term if before the departure of the tenants for their native country China should require the said ground for her own use one month's previous notice to that effect will be given to the tenants who will then give up possession of it without the least hindrance. Having regard to the relations between Chinese and foreigners this step is taken to meet the existing circumstances of the case and it should not be regarded as a precedent in future. This Agreement of rent is therefore drawn up in quadruplicate both in English and Chinese, the British Consul, the local authorities, the gentry and the directors of the 'Wun Chang Kung' temple and the tenants each keeping one copy as proof. As the above mentioned land which was at first rented from W'ANG CHEANG SHANG and his son W'ANG HO SHANG, chair bearers by trade, has on enquiry been found to be Government property, which they had let by means of false deeds, the above mentioned Agreement of Rent has therefore been made without reluctance and the false deeds seven in number given by W'ANG CHEANG SHANG and the others are now given up to the local authorities to be destroyed.

(Signed) JOHN WOLFE.

Tung Chi 5th year 8th moon, 4th day.
September, 1866.

Seal of H.B.M. Consul.
Seal of the
Hau Kwan
District Magistrate.

15.—The piece of land mentioned in the said last hereinbefore mentioned agreement is now in the possession of the defendant and certain buildings have been erected by him and are still standing thereon.

16.—In or about the month of August, 1867, an "Agreement of Rent" in the Chinese language was entered into between the defendant and the Directors of the Taou Shan Kwan temple, translation of which is as follows:—

"Agreement of Rent. The British missionary JOHN R. Wolfe agrees with the Directors of the Taou Shan Kwan temple to rent from them the following property, which was formerly in the 30th year Tau Kwan rented by the missionaries WELTON and JACKSON—namely two houses situated respectively at the back and at the front of the left hand side of the Taou Shan Kwan [these two houses are as follows] 1. One five roomed house with an out house and some waste ground at back and front. 2. One four roomed house at the back with an out house having an upper storey and a lower storey of one room and a piece of waste ground. The rent of the above to be as of old $100 per annum. Also (Mr. WOLFE agrees) to rent the following property, which was originally rented in the fifth year Hsien Feng to the missionaries WELTON and FEARNLEY, namely, Four rooms on the right hand side of the Taou Shan Kwan going straight in: The rent to be as of old $20 per annum. Also a small piece of land formerly hired under a verbal agreement by the missionary GEORGE SMITH: The rent to be as of old $12 per annum. These amount in all to a yearly sum of $132, the first instalment of which for the summer quarter, viz., $33 to be paid at once to the Trade Committee for transmission through the Directors of the Temple to the Taouist priests to be used in the service of the Temple. It is agreed that the same sum be paid quarterly, in advance, according to the English Calendar, to the Trade Committee for transmission, and the rent be not allowed to get into arrears Should this happen, the Directors may let the place to some one else. On the other hand if the rent does not get into arrears the place may not be let to any one else Both parties being of the same mind neither of them can withdraw. It is therefore considered advisable to draw up this agreement in triplicate to be kept by the different parties.

Guarantor—Consul SINCLAIR.
Dated August, 1867.

(Signed) CHOW TAOU WEN. } Directors of the
(Signed) LIN YUNE CHIN. } Taou Shan Kwan.
(Signed) JOHN R. WOLFE.

Seal of Han Kwan Magistrate. British Consular Seal.

17.—The said CHOW TAOU WEN and LIN YUNE CHIN are dead.

18.—No one of the houses mentioned and particularly described in the said last mentioned Agreement of Rent was in actual existence at the date thereof, but the defendant who was at the said time in possession of the buildings which had been substituted for the said houses under the terms of the agreements of 1850 and 1855 herein before appearing, remained and still remains in possession thereof as well as of the piece of land formerly let to the Reverend GEORGE SMITH and has paid rent for the same.

19.—In or about the year 1871 the house which has been built in lieu of one of those leased as aforesaid in 1850 to Messieurs JACKSON and WELTON, and which had been occupied as a residence by the defendant or other missionaries, caught fire and was burnt; and the defendant erected in its stead a much more extensive and lofty structure, and in so doing encroached on land belonging to the said Temple other than that leased to him and destroyed and removed a large rock. In so doing he acted without right or authority. The defendant is still in possession of the said last mentioned house.

20.—In constructing a gateway and entrance road to the said house the defendant has interfered with and blocked up an ancient right of way.

21.—In or about the 3rd moon of the 2nd year of Kwang-Shü (1867) the defendant without any proper license or authority erected an enclosing wall which, commencing on the north side of the said house occupied as a residence by the Missionaries, extended to the West side of the Hill and enclosed together with a portion of the ground leased to him by the said Agreement of 1867 other ground wrongfully claimed by him under the said Agreement.

22.—Complaint having been made to the local authorities by the gentry of Foochow with reference to the said wall, the matter was referred to the British Consul, and by his directions the said wall was pulled down.

23.—In the same year and shortly after the demolition of the said wall the defendant without any proper license or authority erected another wall following the same direction as, but built on a line considerably within, that previously followed by the first mentioned wall. This wall, which is still in existence, wrongfully encloses together with a portion of the ground leased to him by the Agreement of 1867 other ground and several famous and memorial rocks standing thereon wrongfully claimed by him under the said Agreement.

24.—During the year 1878 the defendant without any proper license or authority proceeded to erect on ground enclosed within the said wall to which he wrongfully lays claim under the said Agreement of 1867 a lofty and prominent structure of foreign design. Against this act of encroachment the gentry and inhabitants of Foochow complained to the local authorities and the matter was referred to the British Consul. Negotiations ensued and certain terms of arrangement which had been arrived at were referred to the High Authorities in England for final settlement. Pending such settlement, however, the defendant, wrongfully and in breach of good faith, proceeded with the works upon the said building, and when the same were nearly completed the building was burnt by a mob. The walls however are still standing, and the defendant still claims to hold the land on which they stand under the provisions of the Agreement of Rent of August, 1867.

25.—The plaintiffs allege that the system of ever recurring acts of encroachment and breaches of agreement with reference to the hereinbefore mentioned lands and the buildings standing and being thereon hereinbefore narrated, have heretofore led to great troubles and to collisions between the inhabitants of Foochow and the missionaries of the English Church Missionary Society located at Wu Shih Shan; and they fear and have good cause to fear that unless the rights of the several parties interested in the said lands and premises be ascertained and declared by the decree of this Honourable Court as hereinafter prayed, the future dealings of the defendant with the said lands and premises will give rise to further troubles.

The Plaintiffs therefore pray:—

1.—That the rights of the parties interested therein, in and under the lease of September 1866 hereinbefore set forth, may be ascertained and declared.

2.—That the agreement of Rent dated August 1867 between the defendant and the said CHOW TAO WEN and LIN-YUNE CHIN deceased may be declared and decreed to be void.

3.—That it may be ordered and decreed that the defendant has by his unauthorized and wrongful dealings with the lands premises and buildings leased or purporting to be leased by the agreement of August 1867 forfeited all his right and title in and to the said lands premises and buildings.

4.—That the rights of the parties interested in the Agreement of August 1867 may be ascertained and declared and that the duration of the term of defendant's tenancy and the nature thereof may be ascertained and prescribed.

5.—That the boundaries of the land leased or purporting to be leased t the defendant by the agreement of August 1867 may also be ascertained and declared.

6.—That the plaintiffs may have such further and other relief as the nature of the case may require.

T. C. HAYLLAR,
Counsel for the Plaintiffs.

The answer of JOHN R. WOLFE, the above named defendant, to the amended petition of the above named Plaintiffs.

In answer to the said amended petition I, John R. Wolfe, say as follows:—

1.—I do not know whether the allegations contained in the 1st paragraph of the said amended petition are true or not.

2.—I admit the allegations in the 2nd paragraph of the said amended petition, with the exc pti n of my being the resp nsible head of the English Church Missionary Society at Foochow, which epithet of responsible I do not understand.

3.—I deny the statements in paragraph 3 of the said amended petition.

4.—I admit that in or about the month of December, 1850, the missionaries Welton and Jackson did, with the knowledge and sanction of the Chinese Magistrate for the Haukwan district, rent from a certain Taouist priest the premises at Wu Shih Shan described in the 4th paragraph of the amended petition. I do not admit that the agreement dated the 18th December, 1850, is correctly set out or the premises correctly described, but crave leave to refer to the same when produced at the hearing of this cause and I put the plaintiffs to the proof of their allegation that the said Messrs. Welton and Jackson were the representatives of the Church Missionary Society.

5.—I admit the statements in the 5th paragraph of the amended petition.

6.—In answer to the 6th paragraph of the amended petition I admit that in the year 1855 the Missionaries Fearnley and Welton did agree to rent four rooms in the Taou Shan Kwan Temple, but I deny that they did so without the consent or knowledge of any one authorised in that behalf and I put the plaintiffs to the proof of their allegation that the said Messrs. Fearnley and Welton represented the Church Missionary Society at Foochow.

7.—In answer to paragraph 7 of the amended petition I deny that the said Missionaries did alter and extend the said premises by adding other rooms below.

8.—I admit that the Rev. George Smith did rent from a priest of the said temple a piece of land contiguous to the said temple, as stated in the 8th paragraph of the amended petition, but I deny that either the said George Smith or the lessor had no authority to rent the said land and I deny that the boundaries of the said piece of land have always been in dispute before the filing of the plaintiffs' petition. On the contrary I say that the said boundaries have always been well defined, admitted, and recognised by the lessors.

9.—I admit that I arrived in Foochow in the year 1862 and that since about the year 1863 in the month of September I have had the management of the property at Wu Shih Shan, the subject matter of this suit, and that I have endeavoured to arrange for its absolute conveyance free from the payment of rent.

10.—I deny the statements made in paragraph 10 of the amended petition, but I say that I believe that about the time therein mentioned the said Taouist priest Chun Yuen Ching offered to sell to me a small house called the Blind Man's Temple, but I never paid him any money, nor did I obtain any document from him.

11.—As to the 11th paragraph of the amended petition I say that about the time therein mentioned the said priest told me that he had the permission of the proper authorities to sell the grounds and buildings occupied by the missionaries. I consented to purchase the same if the deeds were duly sealed and stamped by the proper authorities and the property legally transferred. The price agreed upon was considerably over $500, but $500 was paid by me to the said priest as part of the purchase money. The remainder was to be paid by me as soon as the Chinese authorities had stamped the deeds. The necessary deeds were drawn up by the said priest and sent through Her Britannic Majesty's Consul at Foochow to the proper Chinese officers. After two or three months they were returned to the Consul with the message that the priest had no authority to sell the property. I thereupon demanded of the said priest the sum of $500 which I had previously paid to him, but he said he had spent the money and could not refund it, but promised to do so at some subsequent time and in the meanwhile offered to allow the ordinary rent of the premises to remain in my hands as interest on the $500.

12.—In answer to paragraph 12 of the amended petition I say that I do not know if the document therein set forth is correctly quoted and I crave leave to refer to the same when produced at the hearing of this cause and I say that the last preceding paragraph of my answer contains the true account of what took place. The said priest absconded and I deny that he was punished as in the 11th paragraph mentioned.

13.—In answer to paragraph 13 of the amended petition I admit that I did make an application to be allowed to erect a wall and gate in order to keep out beggars and others, but I do not know whether that application is truly set out in the said paragraph and I crave leave to refer to the same when produced on the hearing of this cause and I say that I obtained the leave and license I applied for to erect the wall and gate as they now stand.

14.—I admit that, as stated in the 14th paragraph of the amended petition, an agreement to rent some land for building purposes close to the Wan Chang Kung Temple was, in or about the month of September, 1866, entered into between myself and others of the English Church Missionary Society and the local authorities, but I do not admit that the said agreement is correctly set out in the said 14th paragraph and I crave leave to refer to the said agreement when produced at the hearing of the cause.

15.—I admit the statements in the 15th paragraph of the amended petition.

16.—I admit the statements in the 16th paragraph of the amended petition.

17.—I do not know if the statement in the 17th paragraph of the amended petition is true or not.

18.—I admit the statements in the 18th paragraph of the amended petition.

19.—I admit that the residence as described in the 19th paragraph of the amended petition was burnt down, but it was in 1870. I deny that I erected in its stead a much more extensive structure or that I encroached on land other than that leased to me. I state that the existing house covers less ground than the one burnt down in 1870. And the rock removed had no characters on it and was always inside the verandah of the old house and I say that I had full authority to do what I did.

20.—In answer to the 20th paragraph of the amended petition I say that if any right of way ever existed the gateway and entrance road mentioned in the said 20th paragraph were constructed in accordance with the leave and license granted to me by the proper authorities.

21.—In answer to the 21st paragraph of the amended petition I deny that I wrongfully inclosed any space of ground to which I was not entitled.

22.—I admit that the said wall mentioned in the 22nd paragraph of the amended petition was pulled down.

23.—I deny the statements in the 23rd paragraph of the amended petition except that I admit that I did re-erect a wall which had been partly pulled down and I admit that this wall is still in existence.

24.—In answer to the 24th paragraph of the amended petition I admit that a college was, with the sanction of Her Britannic Majesty's Consul at Foochow, and without visible objection on the part of the plaintiffs or any other persons, erected during the year 1878 on a piece of land enclosed within the said wall. I admit that the said building was burnt by a Chinese mob after the same was completed externally and that I claim the land on which the said building was erected under the agreement of 1867. I deny the other statements in the said 24th paragraph.

25.—In answer generally to the complaints in the amended petition respecting the conduct and dealings of the defendant and the other missionaries who have arranged to rent land and houses at Wu Shih Shan since the year 1850 down to the present time, I say that the most complete good faith has been kept by myself and the other missionaries with the priests and gentry and directors of the temple and other persons who have professed to have authority to cede land to us at Wu Shih Shan, that the lessors have accepted rent from us after having witnessed all we had done, and up to the month of August, 1867, the directors of the temple have distinctly acquiesced in all our building proceedings by deliberately confirming them by the agreement set out in the 16th paragraph of the amended petition, and in September, 1866, by making another agreement as set out in the 15th paragraph of the amended petition, that if by any accident there has been any encroachment, which I deny even to the smallest extent, the same has been wholly unintentional on the part of myself or any of the said missionaries and entirely unproductive of the slightest loss or damage to the plaintiffs. And I submit that inasmuch as the plaintiffs have throughout stood by and witnessed all the building operations of myself and other missionaries at Wu Shih Shan, including the erection of the walls mentioned in the amended petition and more particularly the buildings referred to in the 24th paragraph of the amended petition, which the mob destroyed, without making objection during the progress of the works or until the same were completed, as to the said last mentioned building externally and as to the others in every particular, they are not entitled to complain of any encroachment, supposing any to exist, and they are not entitled to complain of the same as breaches of agreement, even supposing them to be so, which I deny.

26.—I deny all the allegations of the amended petition not specifically alluded to in this my answer.

Mr. Hayllar, in opening his case, read the petition and answer, and proceeded—The question which stands in the very foreground of this case, as it seems to me, is—what is the title of the persons who, under the agreement of 1867 purport to be the lessors of the property in question. Now, we state in the first paragraph of our petition that the Taou Shan Kwan Temple is public property—it belongs in point of fact to the whole City of Foochow—and without the consent of the City of Foochow or persons duly authorised in that behalf the land was let to the defendant. And it is very doubtful whether there is any one authorised in that behalf at all, any one who can pretend to deal with the lands or buildings. Of course, as standing in the relation of landlords to the defendant, our position in this case is accurately and well defined, because he has paid rent to us, and therefore our title to stand here and ask for the relief which we have asked for is quite clear and perfectly valid. But the title of the lessors themselves, and therefore the title the defendant can derive through us to this property, is a question of an entirely different colour.

Now, in the first instance, this Taou Shan Kwan Temple is, as its name implies, a Taouist temple. It is an ancient temple—not very ancient, perhaps, as things go in China—but still an old foundation, if we may so call it, and how it came there and all about it are matters contained in the records of the city and of the temple and public documents generally. It appears that the site on which the temple stands was, towards the end of the Ming dynasty, the private property of a man of considerable reputation, learning, and dignity in the city and it descended to his posterity. His posterity, a few years afterwards, towards the beginning of the present dynasty, in order to commemorate the virtues and the dignities of this deceased scholar, dedicated it to the city. They gave it up to the public, whereupon the public, in gratitude for this dedication and also to commemorate the memory of the same man, by public subscription obtained throughout the city, and probably throughout the province, built these temples which are now standing. From time to time, as the buildings fell into disrepair, further subscriptions were raised throughout the city and province, and also from time to time—and this is of very considerable importance—further temples have been built, and on that ground the city has a perfectly clear right to build further temples still. I put it to your Lordship as one of the first points in this case, that it is in opposition to the fundamental customs and laws of this empire, that property once dedicated to a whole city can in any way be alienated from its original constitution in such a way as to deprive the city of the right of using that land for the purpose for which it was originally dedicated, and that, in this case, there is a right to extend their temple property to the limits of the land if they wish.

Now, how has this property been managed? The property has been managed in a way peculiarly Chinese. It is subject to a certain extent to the control of certain associations. These associations are simply clubs, more or less attached to the services of the different temples, and they get their designations from certain classes of services to which they dedicate themselves. Your Lordship will see the importance of this presently when I point out to you to what purpose the money of the Church Missionary Society was dedicated. It was dedicated to the service of the Temple in providing "incense and lamps," as under another lease also the money was dedicated to the service of "respect for written papers." In 1867 there were about nine of these voluntary associations connected with the Taou Shan Kwan Temple. These associations are, as I have already explained briefly to your Lordship, merely voluntary associations. The members are elected by each other, and their connection with the association depends upon the will of the other members, the payment of their subscriptions, or their own wish to keep up or decline further connection with it. No man has any official connection with it whatever. They are shifting, fluctuating bodies of persons who, as we should say, combine for pleasure rather than religion, because these services partake chiefly of the nature of theatrical performances and feasts. These persons associate themselves in the services of the temples in various ways, and for various objects, such as the association for providing incense and lamps, the association for providing artificial flowers, an association of worshippers, an association for the respect of written papers, and various other associations connected more or less with the worship of the gods, but a great deal more, I presume, with the social life of the Chinese. Some of them have a little property, some are entirely dependent on voluntary subscriptions, and it is their business to supply the wants of the temple as they arise; and in return for this they are entitled to the use of certain rooms in the temple when they go there two or three times a year.

Now a Taouist temple is open at all times to all comers; it is emphatically a public institution; every person is at perfect liberty to go, unmolested by the directors, priest, or anyone else, and perform his religious duties and worship there if he wishes to. The Taou Shan Kwan Temple is regarded as a very sacred one in the city and at certain stated times it is greatly resorted to by worshippers having no connection with the associations. With regard to the associations they have no connection between themselves. The association for the respect of written papers, for instance, has no connection with the association for supplying incense and lamps. They have no joint foundation. Each association is self-managing, their management being subject entirely to their own wishes and according to their own rules, and to carry out their management they elect certain persons whose official title we translate directors. The words "directors of the Taou Shan Kwan Temple" convey a misapprehension. The exact position of these persons is that of directors of the associations connected with the temple, and it is to these associations the temple looks at such times as it has different needs to have them supplied. They look to each of them not only to give them their assistance in supplying the direct needs of the temple but also in obtaining from time to time, as necessity arises, funds for repairing the structures or building fresh temples if required. Such is the actual position of the directors with regard to this temple. Title other than that which is stated in the first paragraph of the petition they in fact have none. It is not a title to the land in any sense in which we understand a title. They do not form a corporation, nor a chapter, nor are they connected in the slightest way with the ownership of the soil, which they have only the part use of by the licence of custom and the unwritten laws of China, which direct all these things. They have that licence to use the premises and to deal in a certain way with the funds they themselves supply.

His Lordship—Are they trustees?

Mr. Hayllar—No; they are not trustees in any way. There is no trust conveyed in their appointment at all. When your Lordship has before you the evidence I shall call, the evidence of the directors themselves and the evidence of their records, you will see how perfectly clear their position is.

Then it will at once be said: "How did these people come to let the land?" Thereby hangs a tale. Your Lordship may ask why I have taken the trouble of tracing the title of the missionaries and their connection with this beautiful piece of property at Wu Shih Shan from 1850, instead of commencing with the lease of 1867? I answer, because it was impossible to convey to your Lordship's mind the slightest apprehension of the real position of the parties relatively without commencing the story *ab initio*. I trace the property from 1850 through the lease of 1855, through certain dealings in regard to it by Mr. Wolfe in 1866, some of which came to nothing but one of which came to a good deal—I trace it through the dealing with a piece of contiguous property in August, 1866, down to August, 1867, when the lease or agreement of rent was entered into between Mr. Wolfe and the deceased directors of two of these associations. Now, leaving for a moment the question of the title of the lessors, I come to consider what is the position of the lessees. When we come to consider a little the legal position of the parties under these documents, it will be a matter for very grave consideration, supposing your Lordship should not hold—as I think I shall show you sufficient reasons for holding—this lease of 1867 to be altogether a void document for various reasons, whether, when your Lordship comes to make a decree you must not hold it void first of all upon the title of the lessors, and next upon the title of the lessees. Now in the lease of 1867, set out in paragraph 16, there is no date for the commencement or termination of the agreement and there is no period by reference to which the latter date can be determined. For example, if a man makes an agreement of this kind and his own tenure is derived from an agreement, for a lease for a term of years the matter then is distinct in equity, although the common law would scarcely go into such a question; but his position is at once clear in equity on the plain ground that there is a period to which the court can refer as being the period which was inferentially imported into the document itself. But in this case, as your Lordship sees, no date is inferentially imported into the document.

Now the lessee appears on the face of the document to be a missionary, John R. Wolfe, but is that its real meaning? I shall call your attention to what I think is the strongest evidence that that is not the meaning, by turning to paragraph 12 of the petition, which sets out that singular agreement which is called a "note of borrowing," and which doubtless expresses the true intent of Mr. Wolfe at the time he received that "note of borrowing" and at the time he made the agreement of rent set out in the 11th paragraph; that was the true intent which was imported into the document when Mr. Wolfe put his signature to it in August, 1867. The special clause to which I refer is "None of the missionaries, whoever they may be, shall, after the return of Mr. Wolfe to England, be called upon to pay rent."

Mr. Hannen said he thought Mr. Hayllar ought not to read half a sentence.

Mr. Hayllar said he would read anything his learned friend wished, but what he had read was a whole sentence.

Mr. Hannen said the following sentence ought to be read, "If the priest wish to collect the rent it is proper the loan shall be refunded."

Mr. Hayllar—I don't think that affects the subject. What I put to your Lordship is that the clear intention of the parties as expressed in this document must be imported into so obscure a document as the lease of 1867. I put it that the agreement was meant to enure to the benefit of all the missionaries as they come to China and, in point of fact, if it could so enure, to the benefit of the Church Missionary Society. Well, in our petition we have said nothing about the Church Missionary Society or its position, for the simple reason that we did not know it. The answer is equally silent. Some proof I shall be able to give to show your Lordship that the Church Missionary Society is nothing in law. It is a fluctuating body of subscribers, having no incorporated position, having no entity. It is very much in the condition of these directors, who are not in a position to hold land, and it can only hold land in England by means of trustees. Now that being the case, it seems to me that if the true intent as expressed in this document is to be carried out, the decree would have to take a completely impossible form and would, in point of fact, have to provide that this property had been let to somebody else not in existence, not born, certainly not in China, of whom we know nothing, in the event of the present gentlemen who are connected with the society going away. That I understand to be the meaning of the note of borrowing set out in paragraph 12; that I understand to be the position the Missionary Society take up. Therefore, dealing with these two points, in the first place, it seems to me that the lease, if it means anything more than what I shall presently contend it does, was void *ab initio* for want of title on both sides, certainly for want of title in the lessors to alienate landed property in any such way as to prevent their instantly resuming it for the purpose for which the temple lands were dedicated to the public.

His Lordship—Are you the representatives of the lessors?

Mr Hayllar—We are here as the receivers of the rent. We are the directors of the temple through whom under this agreement of 1867 the rent is transmitted. That is our position. If we have no title there is no title at all in anybody. As I drew the petition that difficulty struck my mind and therefore I made as parties to the petition the gentry of the city. It pleased Mr. Mowat to strike them out.

Mr. Hannen—I beg your pardon, you consented.

Mr. Hayllar—It was a consent like the consent of these people to the missionaries living in their Temple—it was a consent I could not avoid. It was very late at night and—

His Lordship—Was it near dinner time?

Mr. Hayllar—It was near a much more important time than that; it was near the time of Mr. Mowat's departure. At any rate, the petition was amended and my learned friend is the person entirely responsible for having the gentry struck out. He did not like the look of it for some reason, and against their being there he made a good many objections, and I had not time to open to Mr. Mowat all the difficulties of the position and all the facts in relation to the title of these gentry. At any rate, it was my learned friend who gave the impulse to Mr. Mowat which resulted in my consent to the gentry disappearing from the scene. They have disappeared now, and we will have to deal with the matter as we best can with the directors. My impression all along was that the property was really vested in the representatives of the city. In 1866, when we mad a more formal document, the representatives of the city, the gentry as it is the fashion to call them, who have the control of public affairs in all Chinese cities, were made parties to that agreement. In this case the interests of the city in this agreement are not represented, which is one of the reasons for which, *qua* lease, the lease is void. As an agreement on the part of one set of gentlemen to subscribe to the services of the temple, and on the part of the other side to give these gentlemen the right to dwell within the temple precincts for a short time—treating it in that way—I have no doubt the thing is sufficient, but as a matter of title it is not.

His Lordship—Could the two gentlemen mentioned in the 17th paragraph have been brought in the suit? Could they have instituted this suit?

Mr. Hayllar—I think they could, but I may just explain here, a little out of place, that we do not ask for any order with reference to the land. We are not asking as a remedy that your Lordship should turn these gentlemen out. We are asking for the meaning of an agreement. It is with reference to land and the defendant has recognised our position with reference to the land by paying us the rent, and as he has paid us the rent it does not lie in his mouth to say we are not the proper persons to receive rent, because it is one of the fundamental doctrines of the law of landlord and tenant that the tenant cannot dispute the landlord's title. I was more indifferent therefore than I otherwise should have been to the gentry disappearing. But we now ask, as the persons who receive the rent that we should know how we stand. Your Lordship will see that one of the peculiarities of this case is that the Taouist priest of the temple is the man who first lets the same property which is let in 1867 by the directors. The question is, how did that come about? Had the Taouist priest a better title, or any title, or was it because the priest had no title that the directors were substituted? It happens that the Taouist priest had no title to begin with. The missionaries were placed in this place, not with the consent of the people or the true owners of the ground, but because of the extreme difficulty of providing any location for gentlemen who came here for excellent purposes, but purposes which happen to be in opposition to the wishes of the people of the city, at any rate that class of the people who have the direction of affairs in their hands. To get rid of this difficulty, the missionaries are placed there by the authorities, to enjoy a temporary residence, and the idea was, no doubt, that these gentlemen should go on quietly occupying these two little native houses. Special permission was given to them to alter the inside of the houses and make repairs, but the first thing that must strike your Lordship's mind on reading the document itself is that it was never intended that the property should be turned into a sort of estate, such as it is now, enclosed, with foreign buildings of value upon it, schools, and garden, and so on. That was not the original idea of the thing; it is the good nature of the people that has allowed that to be done. My learned friend says we have acquiesced. We have acquiesced because people do acquiesce in that which they can't particularly help; and also because among people who are numerically very large, as the city of Foochow is—according to the Rev. Justus Doolittle the population of the city is 600,000—it is nobody's special business to prevent these things. So far as we have not prevented them we do not ask for any relief from your Lordship's Court. I thought at first, that the Haukwan District Magistrate had given the missionaries a title to this property. My learned friend puts it with complete accuracy in his 4th paragraph that the missionaries did, "with the knowledge and sanction of the magistrate, rent from a certain Taouist priest," and that is what it legally comes to, although if we probed the business to the bottom we should find that even that was not quite right.

We have seen a good deal recently of the way these things are managed. These cases take to a certain extent the form of negotiation between the two Governments. Where missionaries have to be provided with locations it forms the subject of a good deal of negotiation which goes on through despatches, which, I think, throw much light upon the subject. In this instance neither the Taouist priest nor the directors are in the position of private people wanting to let their property, who in their minds acquiesce in what is going on, because of course if a man were a perfectly voluntary agent, as we understand the term in England, and then said he had let a thing to which he had no title, why, it would be a sort of allegation the court would not pay much attention to. But that is not the attitude of these people. They did not want this place to be let; they were and are much averse to it. I don't suppose the Taouist priest was, because he benefited by the transaction; it converted him from a person in receipt of a very small pittance to one in receipt of a much larger pittance. Well, the Tauoist priest is a person who is appointed by the directors of these associations. He is their servant. He is a person who has no connection with the property of the temple himself, which I believe in Buddhist temples and monasteries the priests to a certain extent have. But the Taouist priest is the mere servant of the public, appointed by the directors who have the management of the temple and who pay him, not exactly a salary, but certain sums to perform certain duties; that is to say, as in this particular case of the rent under the lease of 1867, the money has to be transmitted to him for the purpose of being employed in certain services of the temple. It was not to go into the Taouist priest's pocket, nor the pockets of the directors, but through an indirect process it was finally to enure to the benefit of the Taouist priest. Probably he would be the person most interested in the money part of the transaction. It is no benefit to the directors; it is no benefit to the city, and they don't want it. It really does go to the priest; therefore, I have no doubt, he is a more pliant instrument in the hands of people wanting to make bargains than anyone else, so we see that in the agreement of 1850 the Taouist priest is the person who stands forward in the light of the landlord. Your Lordship will perceive there that he lets certain rooms—one house with five rooms in a row broadwise, to which was attached an outhouse and a yard at back and front, which I believe is attached to all Chinese houses—a small place for the chopping of wood and drying of clothes; one house of four rooms, to which was attached an outhouse having an upper storey of two rooms and a lower storey of one room.

Mr. Hannen said he denied the correctness of the translation as to that.

Mr. Hayllar—Well, that is our translation, which we shall support. It was agreed that the rent should be $100 per annum, that the rent should be paid in advance every three months, according to the English calendar, that the Taouist priest should not interfere with or obstruct any works going on or repairs *inside* the houses, which were to be done at the expense of the lessees; that it should be at the option of the lessees to continue—or to discontinue I think I should add—the tenancy, words which, as your Lordship will see, are most significantly omitted from the lease of 1867; and that the Taouist priest should not be at liberty to let the premises to other persons. I may as well state at once that in the lease of 1867, although the property had been altered and was not at all in the condition it was in when the lease of 1850 was made, so far from acquiescing in what had been done, we redescribed the property in the same terms as we described it in the lease of 1850. That has great significance as to what we understood was going to happen. We don't use the fact as any proof that the place has been forfeited, but as showing the intention and understanding of the parties that the property was at a certain time to be given up in the same state in which it was in 1850. That is in accordance with Chinese law. I believe that if, all over China, a man alters property, that circumstance does not of itself work a forfeiture as it does with us. In England to alter property, even to improve it, against the will of the owner, is, as every one knows, to commit waste or as it is termed *devastavit*; and to use a house for one purpose when it is let for another, as, for instance to convert it into a mill, has the same effect, and the party so offending would be liable to be turned out. According to Chinese law that would not be the case, but on the property being given up it would have to be given back again in the same condition as it was in before. That being in the minds of the parties is the reason why the property was redescribed in the same words as in the lease of 1850.

Then in 1855 another small piece of land was let to the missionaries who then represented the society, that is to say, to Messrs. Fearnley and Welton, by another priest. At that time Lin Yung Mow had either gone away or died. I believe he was dead, but at any rate his connection with the temple was severed, and then Chun Yuen Ching, who had been all the time at the temple in his pupilage but in 1855 had been appointed to the position of the priest of the temple, let this property to Messrs. Fearnley and Welton. Now it seems to me that so far as the lease of 1850 was concerned the severance of the connection of Lin Yung Mow with the temple really voided that document. However, that is not of very great importance at this moment. There was another piece of land let to Mr. Smith, of which I shall have to say someting presently.

But now we come to the dealings of Mr. Wolfe, the very energetic and able gentleman who came to China in the year 1862 or 1863. Between 1850 and 1855 and 1863 circumstances had very much changed. This piece of ground, which was when first let purely a piece of temple property, by this time had assumed an entirely different aspect, and it had consequently become of very great importance to the missionary society that their title should receive some higher sanction than it had hitherto received. By 1865 it had become a valuable piece of property on account of their schools, or chapels, and it was of great importance to them that they should be located where they were, that they should not be moved, and we then find, what is in accordance with this state of things, the operations which Mr. Wolfe commenced. My learned friend need not suppose I intend to cast the slightest slur on Mr. Wolfe for what he did. He had but recently come to the country; he would see that the Taouist priest was the lessor under the lease of 1850, and it would be of extreme importance to the missionaries to find themselves there with a title good against the world, one which would allow them to deal with the premises as they pleased, and under which they would not be liable to be turned out at any time when the property happened to be wanted by the Chinese. Your Lordship will now understand why these documents are inserted in the petition, because it was on account of these dealings with the priest that the directors came to the conclusion, as we shall presently see, that the priest could not be trusted. As long as he simply let the property for temporary purposes, merely to allow these gentlemen to live in the place and use the premises for a residence it was not of much importance, but when they came to understand how Mr. Wolfe regarded his position and when they saw that it was not intended that this property should not be used simply as a residence for the gentlemen, but was to be turned into a sort of permanent missionary location, then their eyes were opened. A matter which had been at first of little importance had become in 1865, in consequence of what had been done by the previous missionaries, and the intentions of Mr. Wolfe, as shown by the documents of the priest, of great significance.

I must now refer for one moment to the answer, and in reference to this paragraph I think there must have been a slip of memory on the part of Mr. Wolfe in his answer, probably arising from the length of time which has elapsed. We set out that a document was entered into by which he got the property conveyed to him for the consideration of $800 on a perpetual lease.

I would for a moment here interrupt myself to explain what I mean by a perpetual lease. I am, of course, not familiar with these matters myself, but I have heard a good deal about them during the last two months, and I think the words "yung yuen," having the meaning of perpetuity, are used wherever private property is transferred from one person to another, the purchaser being a foreigner. They are well understood by the Chinese and have the same meaning as a document conveying by an absolute assignment by sale. I believe among the Chinese themselves, and it is possible also sometimes in dealing with foreigners, they use another expression for absolute conveyance. I will give you the word from a gentleman who was formerly Prefect of this District and who has come from Peking to explain all he knows about this matter. I forget what the word is, but there is an expression which means absolute conveyance, but, as your Lordship knows, all property in China is vested by the fundamental constitution of the empire in the Emperor himself. All except two classes of land therefore are subject to rent. The two exceptions are temple lands and grave yards. When property is conveyed by a Chinaman to a foreigner, therefore, I believe more from a feeling of pride than anything else, instead of "absolute assignment" the term "perpetual lease" is used, because nearly all lands are subject to rent. In the settlement, where we have built on a grave yard, no rent is reserved to the crown; also on temple lands, the crown foregoes its right for purposes which it considers so sacred. As I understand, in China the woods "yung yuen" convey the idea of perpetuity and when they are used a seller practically gives up his rights then and there. I believe it is the same in Shanghai. There is a property there described—wrongly, according to the highest authority in China—as a concession, but there a rent is always reserved to the crown of China, while here, among the graves, property is held without rent. With the exception of the two classes of property, grave yards and temple lands, rent is always reserved to the crown.

His Lordship—They are holders in fee.

Mr. Hayllar—Yes, but the feudal tenure has so long been abolished in China, if it ever existed, that I don't know whether that would convey the meaning.

His Lordship—They are subject to a fee farm rent.

Mr. Hayllar—That is the position. It is the same in India. There the whole of the land is vested in the crown and the ryots all over the country are subject to the payment of taxes. It takes the form of a fee farm rent. In some places it is settled in perpetuity. In China, I believe, the crown reserves to itself the right of altering the rent according to the fertility of the land, making a difference in time of famine, for instance. But throughout China it is not the practice to admit, by the form of document given to foreigners, that the land has been alienated in such a way that it should not pay rent to the crown; although, subject to this small rent it belongs out and out to the purchaser.

There is a peculiar way of dealing with land in China. When a man makes a payment of a sum down he may get a "yung yuen" or another form of conveyance that would answer more correctly to our absolute assignment. But if a man wants to let his property for a term of years he does it by morgage. That, I believe, is universal throughout this province and throughout China. A lump sum is paid down by the mortgagee to the mortgagor, and the mortgagee enters into possession of the property, paying no rent but using it until the period of the mortgage has elapsed. Mortgages are also made for indefinite periods to operate as leases. In that case they answer to our mortgages; that is to say the mortgage money has to be repaid at the end of the period. But in the mortgage I am alluding to the lump sum paid down stands in the place of rent; it goes for the use of the property and is not repaid. The mortgage money is paid down then and there as the rent in one lump sum. Then there is a form of agreement, like the one we have here, which is said by all persons—by my witnesses at any rate—to be a tenancy from year to year, or it may amount to a tenancy from month to month in certain districts, but the important point is this, that there is no such thing in China as a perpetual lease under which an amount payable at stated periods is reserved. As I am informed there is no such document except for a temporary purpose, that is to say, the very fact of the reservation of rent means that it cannot be a lease for more than from year to year or month to month as the case may be; but if once you get rid of the payment of rent, once it can be proved that rent is not paid—and many Chinese tenants are very tricky and often try to get off the payment of rent—then the fact of rent not being paid is a proof there has been either a mortgage or an absolute assignment.

Now, we see at once, the significance of these documents made between the priest and Mr. Wolfe, and the way the Chinese read them. The answer says, in reference to this $800 document, "I deny the statements made in paragraph 11 of the amended petition, but say that I believe about the time therein mentioned the said Taouist priest Chun Yuen Ching offered to sell to me a small house called the Blind Man's Temple, but I never paid him any money nor did I obtain any document from him."

Well, we have a document, which purports to be a lease for a perpetual term, not of the Blind Man's Temple, which is a little temple in the immediate neighbourhood of the Taou Shan Kwan, forming indeed part of it, and which is also in very close contiguity to the property held by these gentlemen, but describing the property in the same terms as it was described in in the leases of 1850 and 1855, and purporting to be a conveyance in perpetuity of that property. It also purports to convey land "on the edge of the road by the wall of the Ne-to'-tsze monastery, and on the right hand thereof (West) on the wall of the Pan-leong-tung monastery." The existence of this document was subsequently found out by the directors themselves. The priest had not communicated to them his intention of dealing with the property in that way, and they heard of it by accident. They got a copy which was at length forwarded to the Haukwan Magistrate, and there it was cancelled. Well, the matter is not of such vast importance in itself. I have not the slightest doubt Mr. Wolfe, when he looks a little more fully into the subject, will be able to throw a little more light upon it. I dare say his memory is now a little overlaid.

But the next document is a curious one by which we find that the property is again let by the same Taouist priest to Mr. Wolfe, for a perpetual term, for $500. My learned friend's answer is a little important on that point. He says "As to the 12th paragraph of the amended petition I say that about the time therein mentioned the said priest told me that he had the permission of the proper authorities to sell the grounds and buildings occupied by the missionaries. I consented to purchase the same if the deeds were duly sealed and stamped by the proper authorities and the property legally transferred. The price agreed upon was considerably over $500, but $500 was paid by me to the said priest as part of the purchase money. The remainder was to be paid by me as soon as the Chinese authorities had stamped the deeds." Now, a curious point about this is, that in the document itself, which was forwarded to us, and of course we can only know about it from that, except from the evidence of the priest, who is here, this perpetual lease purports to be in consideration of $500 only. There is not a word in the lease which says how much more was to be paid. The document is rather a singular one, and I will read to your Lordship the translation we have. After describing the land it goes on—"The rent in former years was paid quarterly, and John Wolfe since his coming here to preach and occupying the premises likewise has been paying the rent quarterly according to the terms, but he feeling very much the annoyance caused by the Taouist priest's repeated calls, pressing for payment of rent, is willing to pay to the said priest $500, in order that he shall never again call to collect any rent; and from henceforth no missionary occupying the premises, whoever he be, shall have to pay any rent, nor any of the priests at the Taou Shan Kwan Temple shall call to collect more rent." There can be no doubt that if that document had been passed this priest would have sold over our heads and over the heads of the whole city this piece of property in perpetuity to the missionaries. It created, naturally, immense indignation, and it subsequently led to the priest being punished for this and being dismissed. Nothing could show more clearly the feeling of the people at that time with reference to the property than the conduct they displayed. We say the matter was referred to the British Consul and being brought before him this lease was ordered to be cancelled, and when I come, as I presently shall, to call your Lordship's attention to the negotiations which took place you will see the extreme importance of these documents as showing the intention of the parties.

We next come to the "note of borrowing," which I have read to your Lordship in the petition and which I shall therefore only refer to, but there is an unfortunate difference between the memory of the priest on this point, and the statement contained in the answer. In the statement contained in the answer Mr. Wolfe says, "The necessary deeds were drawn up by the said priest and sent through Her Britannic Majesty's Consul at Foochow to the proper Chinese officers. After two or three months they were returned to the Consul with the message that the priest had no authority to sell the property. I thereupon demanded of the said priest the sum of $500 which I had previously paid to him, but he said he had spent the money and could not refund it, but promised to do so at some subsequent time, and in the meanwhile offered to allow the ordinary rent of the premises to remain in my hands as interest on the $500." Now the recollection of the priest is that he was not trusted with the $500 before the property was registered, that the facts connected with the $800 lease were before the eyes of the parties, and there was some considerable doubt whether the $500 lease would be registered, and the $500 were not paid any more than the $800 mentioned in the previous document were paid. But on the return of this document, it being then quite hopeless to suppose that the people would submit to the sale of this property, a $500 loan was made to the priest on the security of this document in the month it bears date. The priest's recollection is that the money was paid to him in three distinct sums. Therefore they got round the difficulty which was inherent in the case by not making a sale of the property, but "a note of money borrowed," which was to all intents and purposes the same thing and operated as a perpetual lease; that if it should so happen that affairs could be managed so that rent should not be paid, this $500—which was certainly a very small price for this fine property and was lent at high interest, viz, over 24 per cent. per annum—should exactly cover the rent and never be repaid, and in point of fact the property would be the missionaries'! That is how affairs stood up to August, 1866.

Now, how did the missionaries act under the agreement of the 13th August, 1866? For one quarter they refused to pay the rent, and as far as the real proprietors of the temple were concerned, the people of the city and the directors of the different associations, they knew nothing of the matter, and it was not until it was found out that the rent had not been paid to the priest that the matter was brought to the notice of the gentry in July, 1867. It was then referred to the British Consul, and through him this document came to the knowledge of the directors and it was decreed by these authorities that the rent should be paid as before.

This leads up to the point why the directors were made parties to this document. *They were made parties to this document because they would not trust the priest any more.* He disappeared from the scene and had disappeared altogether until he was recently unearthed, he having concealed himself and changed his religion. However, the directors of the temple, finding how their cherished property was being dealt with, or rather spirited away, said, "We must have a different agreement and the agreement must be made through us," meaning not that the amount should be paid to the directors for themselves, but to them as mere conduit pipes for handing the money to the Taouist priest to be employed in the services of the temple. Moreover, the rent having been refused under the agreement between the priest and Mr. Wolfe of 3th August, 1866, the directors said, "Not only will we ourselves personally interfere, but we will ask the assistance of the British Government in order that the property shall not be so dealt with again." Mr. Sinclair most kindly consented to be the guarantor of the rent and his guarantee was regarded by the Board of Trade, as a security not only that the money should be paid through him, but that the people should be free from any surreptitious dealing with the property in the particular manner I have described, and that the missionaries should not be able to say, "We have a permanent title to the property because we have paid no rent."

As to the rent itself, it is nothing—$ 32 a year for a beautiful place like that is nothing to the city. The directors did not want the money, it was the evidence of the non-payment of the rent which they dreaded. It was the fact that the missionaries were dealing in such a way as would have made their title permanent. That is what they wanted, and that is what we did not want. So your Lordship sees now the reason of the difference between the two agreements. First of all, the rent is to be paid through Mr. Sinclair to the directors, and in the next place we had found out how they were going to deal with us, how the property which had been lent to them as a mere residence had been converted into an estate, that we were not dealing only with two missionary gentlemen then and there, but with a large class coming one after another. In the new lease we left out the only words which would have given them a shadow of permanency, that "it should be at the option of the lessor to continue or discontinue the hiring." These alterations were in fact aimed at what had been done. The agreement of 1867 was made by the people under the light of previous circumstances, which to them were, of course, extremely significant.

At this stage the Court adjourned for tiffin.

On the court resuming Mr. Hayllar continued his address. He proposed to read some passages from documents written by Consul Carroll which led up to the making of the agreement of 1867, but on Mr. Hannen intimating that he should object to their admissibility as evidence, he said he would not interrupt his opening statement by arguing the point now, but would tender the documents in evidence afterwards subject to argument. There were other documents, he said, from Mr. Consul Carroll which had a material bearing on the $500 lease and the punishment of Chun Yuen Ching. He had a document in which Mr. Consul Carroll prayed for the release of the priest. It is said in the answer, he continued, and I think under some misapprehension of what · meant, that the priest was not punished. Well, he was punished, and was released at the instance of the Consul, and shortly afterwards disappeared. Subsequently it was asked that he should be punished, but that was from a different view · f the transaction While they were relying on his title and they thought they could get the premises from him they asked for his release. I don't know that there can be any objection to my reading that document.

His Lordship—As far as I am concerned I think it is immaterial whether the priest was punished or n t.

Mr Hayllar—Then I will not trouble y ur Lordship with that, but what is important in this document is this, "After careful consideration f this matter I see there is no reason why the premises occupied by Mr. Wolfe should not be still rented at a yearly tenancy, though their being rented for a perpetual term is inconsistent with reason." The matter went on, and then came the negotiations between August, 1866, and the lease of 1867, with reference to that lease. These were conducted thr ugh the aut orities entirely on both sides and I think the documents are quite admissible under the rule in equity by which it constantly happens that t e oral negotiations leading up to leases are admitted, and, moreover, I think the admission of these despatches would be only fair to both sides. · don't know whether my friend objects to these.

Mr. Hannen—I do.

His Lordship—Is there any point of importance under the agreement of 1866?

Mr. Hayllar—Not of very great importance, but it is an agreement that cannot be left out of the whole thing. In this case the proper name of the temple is the Wun Chang Kung, but it is a subsidiary part of the Taou Shan Kwan. Then we come now to the document of 1867, and I have shown, as far as I have been permitted to show it how it was led up to and the title of the lessors.

His Lordship—I understand you to say they had no title.

Mr. Hayllar—No title to alienate.

His Lordship—And about leasing?

Mr. Hayllar—Nor to lease.

His Lordship—You say, I think, "We cannot give you anything."

Mr. Hayllar—I don't go so far as that. I say we can give them a licence to live there.

His Lordship—*De anno in annum?*

Mr. Hayllar—Yes. In fact we have done it and are bound by it. What we can give as between ourselves and them I presume we have given, but of course the narrow question is what we could give. The ordinary rule would be that a man cannot derogate from his own grant, but when we find people in the position these people occupied, the point I put to your Lordship is, did they mean to give more than they have, looking at the wording of the document and the position of the parties? The actual relationship of the directors to the temple, it seems to me, throws a complete light on what they meant to give, and that leads me at once to what I have to say about the agreement of 1867.

I have pointed out various things in it, such as that it describes a property which really at that time had no existence, or rather, which had entirely disappeared under the manipulation of the lessees; and that that fact is one which has some significance, the meaning I put upon it being that it was intended the property as described in the lease should revert to the temple in exactly the same state as it had been let in. I have also called your Lordship's attention to the fact that the directors have been substituted for the priest under very peculiar circumstances. The directors have never really treated this money as rent to themselves. I have already said they were merely a conduit of communication between those who were to pay the money and those who were to receive it. Then c mes this, "It is agreed the sum be paid quarterly in advance to the Trade Committee for transmission and the rent be not allowed to get into arrears." That is to say, as I understand the real meaning of the document, until the rent is paid each quarter the title of the lessees does not accrue. It is quite a different thing, the idea being fundamentally different, from leases in England, so that if a man did not pay rent in advance he could be turned out at once, that is to say, the landlord could resume without giving three months' notice to quit. Well, then, according to the custom I think of all China, the option of taking or refusing that rent when tendered lies with the lessors. If a person tenders rent in advance it is open to the lessors under a lease of this kind, if they want to get rid of him, to refuse it; but by the custom of the country, (supposing it to be a lease for a year with a quarterly rent reserved, as in this case—which I don't think is a very common form among the Chinese) if the tenant's rent be refused, he would then be permitted to occupy the premises for three months without rent and then he must go; that is to say, the three months' use of the premises is equivalent, according to the understanding which is perfectly well known to all Chinese, to a three months' notice and is supposed to be a compensation for the expense to which the tenant is put by the removal. In all cases where the rent is payable in advance, the simple plan, instead of giving a notice to quit, which is an English notion, is for the landlord to refuse the tenant's rent when offered. The meaning of it is that if you refuse the rent, if the rent is not paid, the tenant has no title, because his title d es not accrue until the rent is paid. Should the rent not be tendered the landlord may at once resume, that is to say, the man who does not pay the rent loses the privilege he would have had if the landlord had refused it. It works a forfeiture forthwith, and the curious thing is that looking through a vast number of Chinese leases, as I have had to do, I find it does not make any difference even if the rent is paid by the guarantor. Almost all leases have guarantors where the rent reserved is at all considerable, but still, if the tenant does not pay the rent himself and has to resort to the guarantor he has to go without being allowed that privilege of the three months' rent.

Then the agreement goes on—"On the other hand, if the rent does not get into arrears the place may not be let to any one else." The construction put upon that by my learned friend is, as I understand, that that is equivalent to an agreement on our part to let him occupy the property as long as he likes.

His Lordship—He will also contend the directors cannot resume possession for their own occupation.

Mr. Hayllar In point of fact I understand my learned friend's position to be the same as though we had made an agreement in English form not to give a notice to quit.

His Lordship—Or that the tenancy may be continued at his option?

Mr. Hayllar—Yes.

His Lordship—You having no option?

Mr. Hayllar—Yes; that is, as I understand, the contention of the other side, and one of the questions in this case, apart from the title of the two parties, is: what is the meaning of the words "May not let to anyone else?" Now, we say they mean exactly what they say they do, neither more nor less; that they express in the most distinct form what was passing through the minds of the writers, because they occur, I believe, in nearly every lease that is made in this City. The words have to the Chinese a distinct meaning, which passes through the minds of those who enter into these agreements between themselves.

His Lordship—Is this a common form then?

Mr. Hayllar—It is a common form. I believe this document to be one of hundreds of thousands of similar instruments made out by one of the writers who sit at the corners of the streets and make out the documents for a few cash. They are called chong-szes and very often you see the name chong-sze at the bottom of t e document. By the Chinese these chong-szes are not regarded very favourably. The words "may not be let to any one else" have a history. Like a great many expressions in English and in every other language in the world, they have passed from their original into an idiomatic meaning, and the history of it is this, that both landlords and tenants in China being a little tricky in money matters, as soon as a man's property depreciates in value the tenant goes from time to time and offers less rent and if the landlord takes it, the rent is regarded as being thenceforth reduced. But the property may be in a rising neighbourhood and then the first thing the landlord does is to try to raise the rent, although he has agreed not to do so, and in order to carry that out he produces before his tenant a real or fictitious tenant, who immediately offers a higher rent, and by that means the rent is raised. The words, "if the rent does not get into arrears the place shall not be let to any one else," therefore are an idiomatic expression which means "you won't raise the rent." It means that and nothing else, that "we, the tenants, shall not be subject to this treatment, and if you do bring anyone else in in order to raise the rent upon us you won't be successful."

His Lordship—As you say, the real pinch of the case is on these few words.

Mr. Hayllar—Yes, I think so.

His Lordship—The only question is whether the translation is correctly given.

Mr. Hayllar—We fortunately have in this court some very high authorities upon the Chinese language.

Mr. Hannen—I admit the translation in the petition.

Mr. Hayllar—The exact equivalents of the various terms are—"First pay rent, afterwards occupy house, if owe rent let the directors resume or take back and/or rent to others, if not owe rent directors cannot let others." That, I believe, is as literal a translation as the Chinese language will admit of, so that really "the place may not be let to any one else" is a very correct rendering. The land may not be let to any one else, but this does not interfere with what is inherent in every such lease, the right of the landlord to resume for his own purposes, the inference being, in dealing with property of Chinese, that a man would not want to get rid of his tenant. We happen to reverse the position a good deal in this case, but as a rule a man who holds property does so as an investment and does not wish to get rid of a tenant except to let it to somebody else. One of the witnesses I shall call is one of the largest owners of house property in this province. The chances are a hundred to one against his wanting a particular house for his own purposes, but what he would do with it, after his fashion, would be to raise the rent by letting it to somebody else, but if he tried that he would be foiled;

the courts would not admit it. He cannot turn one man out and put in another, a rival in trade or a rival in price. It means that distinctly to the mind of a Chinaman; the chance of his wanting the house himself is so small, except where a man wants a house to set up his son. If a landlord's son were going to be married, under this agreement he would be permitted to resume the property for his own purposes; or if he wanted to open a shop himself he would be permitted to resume for that purpose. If a man wants to put in a stranger to raise the rent it is against the equity of the document; if he wants to put in his son or himself it is in accordance with the equity of the document and, as they put it, the "reason" of the case. The words themselves are so common that they appear, I believe, in almost every document of the kind. When they say the word "choo" which appears in this lease does not create anything more than a mere temporary title. Every arrangement they make for dealing with property for rent is a mere temporary measure, and the whole thing is simply an agreement against a certain form of extortion.

Now in this case there is no doubt the property is let at an extremely moderate rent, a rent which is not in the slightest degree equivalent to the value of the property. The missionaries have had the use of it for a good many years at this rent, and what Mr. Wolfe may have understood by these words I don't pretend to say, because of course I cannot enter into his mind, but one thing would be very natural, that he certainly would not wish the rent raised. *Ex necessitate rei*, I should have thought they would be obscure to Mr. Wolfe's mind if he had not shown himself so very much alive to the importance of the terms as evidenced by the other agreements he made in 1866.

Now, as throwing light on the document of 1867, I wish to call your Lordship's attention to the lease of 1866, which is made between the same parties, and there your Lordship sees that when we were going to deal with property which was to depart out of our possession for a lengthened period of time, with a property which we were admittedly going to allow buildings to be placed upon, we dealt with it in a very different manner and much more serious spirit. It is not to be supposed that the Chinese do these things carelessly; in point of fact I believe there are no people who confer about any dealing with property so vigorously as they do; there is no act which in all its bearings is not discussed. If you come to compare the agreement of 1867 with that of 1866 you will find some very marked distinctions. In the first place the agreement of 1867 is made with Mr. Wolfe, this in itself showing that they regarded it as a temporary agreement made with one man; but the agreement of 1866 is made with "Mr. Wolfe and others of the Church Missionary Society." Now, I don't know exactly who these others are, but it is clear the Chinese understood perfectly well that other persons were coming. They knew that, from what had taken place before, and they became alive to the fact that it was a succession of gentlemen coming one after the other they had to deal with, and they in their fairness of mind treated with Mr. Wolfe on that basis. They say "we are going to let you have it for twenty years, though it is not probable you yourself will be here for twenty years." Whether these words do not invalidate the whole document as making it an uncertainty is a question on which I will have a word or two to say to your Lordship shortly. Knowing that Mr. Wolfe was not likely to remain here so long, they let him have the land. That is a very important consideration. In the one case we say, "We let you have the land as a personal matter; in the other case we treat with your Society." Then they go on, "As they wish to rent a piece of Government Ground," and you see here they specify the nature of the ground, which they do not do in the case of the Taou Shan Kwan ground. It is a very serious step they are entering upon, because one has only to read the history of missionary troubles in China to know from what sources they arise. They arise from the fact that the people regard with such intense jealousy, in consequence of *fung shui* and other reasons, the building of foreign houses in a city. It is liable to raise a storm which Prospero himself could not allay. It is not a matter to be lightly regarded, and they did not regard it lightly. They state that it is Government ground, or rather public ground, in the district of Haukwan, and then they state what it is for—for building purposes. That is a thing which is omitted from the other document. In that case we say they have encroached little by little, being there for so many years unmolested, they having great interest in doing it, and the people not having their own representatives on the spot. On the other hand, when we want to let you a piece of land for building purposes we know perfectly well what we are about and we let you a piece of land for that.

Then we have here an element we have not in previous agreements, we have the gentry. They are people outside the directors with, in fact, a perfectly hostile interest. They say to the directors, "You have no right to have done what you have." There is no unity between them. But in this agreement of 1866 the gentry come forward. "At the request of the Consul the gentry and directors of the said place have been invited to go with them and make a clear inspeoti n of the said piece f land." Now in the agreements of 850 and 1867 there is nothing of that kind; the thing is left in the loosest p ssible way. Why? There ought t have been no mistake. The intention was not that you s ould build walls here and make enclosures there, but that you should occupy a few houses with a little piece of land attac ed, appurtenances, as I apprehend the word would be, properly translated. We let them without describing the boundaries for the simple reason that we never intended t em to be used for anything except what we say they ought to have been used for. But when we intend them to build we g about it in a very different way and have a clear inspection, and t en what is found?

The learned counsel went on to read the boundaries of the land as stated in the lease set out in the petition, and proceeded—Could anything be more accurately and well-done? Why, it is equal to the best deeds we can draw in England, and Chinese are perfectly capable of doing these things themselves w en they know what is wanted, but of course when there is a misapprehension of their intentions there comes confusi n, but here there is no confusion. And what was intended? The houses are to be of a very special description. "The houses to be built thereon will be of the same description as those in the neighbourhood—not detrimental to the position of the neighbouring native houses." That is very important, for I believe according to the fundamental customs of the place a man is not allowed to build a house higher than his neighbour's. Whether this arises originally from the fact that this would keep out light, or allow a family house to be over-looked, or because it would interfere with *fung shui*, the fact remains that any man who did that would have a great chance of being very severely bambooed. And that of course would have been the fate of these gentlemen had they happened to be Chinese. They would not have been allowed to do it for a moment, they would have been subject to punishment, but each one being *civis Romanus* they could not be punished in that way. A Chinese would have had his house pulled down about his ears in a minute. When we intend houses to be built we describe them in this way.

"The ground is rented through Chow Fung Yuen and other gentry and directors of the Wun Chang Kung temple duly appointed." Duly appointed! How? At a public meeting. When they were going to deal in reality with the Government property, then they resort to those means which are known to t em. They did not, in a hole and corner manner, in a corner of the temple, make an agreement with a priest, because there is great jealousy on all these matters in the city, but as they were really going now to give a great privilege they do the best they can; they call a public meeting, and then they grant the land for $15 per annum, which amount is t be handed over to the British Consul for transmission to Chow and other gentry, to be spent in aid of the cause of respect for written papers. Now the distinction between the gentry and directors was taken by me in the petition. It is now out of it, but to those who made this lease it was a very important distinction.

His Lordship—This is a differen trus'.

Mr. Hayllar—It all belongs to he same Taou Shan Kwan Temple, but this particular temple is connected with the cause for the respect of written papers. They are different parts of the same association.

His Lordship—You are now on the agreement of 1866. There is nothing there said about the directors of the Taou Shan Kwan Temple.

Mr. Hannen—We say that is merely descriptive of a particular piece of ground.

Mr. Hayllar—It makes no difference to the argument I am addressing to your Lordship.

His Lordship—How do you show a right to relief in respect to this lease of 8 6?

Mr. Hayllar—Simply as directors of the Taou Shan Kwan.

Mr. Hannen—There is no breach alleged.

Mr. Hayllar—I don't say there is. I am not asking for relief. I am simply asking your Lordship what our position is with regard to it. The property is a piece of the original ground, it is public ground, and is let by the directors of the temple and gentry.

His Lordship— t may be public ground. The only question is whether the plaintiffs are entitled to sue in respect of the agreement of 1866. I don't say they are not: I only put it to you.

Mr. Hayllar—I am aware of the position. The importance of the lease to us is as showing what was done when they were going to build. It is to place before your Lordship's mind, sitting here as a foreigner, dealing with a piece of land in Chinese jurisdiction, the distinction between the cases, showing you how they dealt with the land, and as such it appears to me the best kind of evidence that can be laid before you. It is extremely difficult for me or for your Lordship, as I apprehe d, to place our minds in the same position as those of the parties to this document on one side. The administration of justice, I presume, depends upon our knowledge of a great many things we have to take for granted. The administration of justice by a foreign judge in China must depend on a great many things we cannot take for granted, and in getting at the real meaning of the parties it is necessary to introduce things which would be irrelevant in England or which are only relevant as showing the meaning of the parties. I am using this document as showing the meaning of the parties, not as asking relief with regard to it. "The tenants shall from this date build houses within the boundary as above described, without the least encroachment, and the houses so built shall not be higher than the neighbouring native houses or to the detriment of their positions. As this is Government ground it shall on no account be sub-let to other persons for building houses thereon. It is leased for a term of twenty years; at the expiration of the said term, if before the departure of the tenants for their native country, China should require the said ground for her own use, one month's previous notice to that effect will be given to the tenants, who will then give up possession of it without the least hindrance." Then comes an important clause. "Having regard to the relations between Chinese and foreigners, this step is taken to meet the existing circumstances of the case, and it should not be regarded as a precedent in future." This has, in fact, two meanings; the first is that they have departed from their usual plan in letting ground for a term of years at an annual rent, a sort of tenancy which is unknown in China; in the next place it means that Government ground is not to be regarded as property to be let. It was not to be a precedent for letting Government ground for a term of years, or for letting it at all; the thing is to be quite *sui generis*; it is to stand alone and not to be drawn into a precedent for the future.

Then comes this—"As the above mentioned land, which was at first rented from Wang Cheang Shang and his son Wang Ho Shang, chair bearers by trade, has on inquiry been found to be Government property, which they had let by means of false deeds, the above mentioned agreement of rent has therefore been made without reluctance, and the false deeds, seven in number, given by Wang Cheang Shang and the others are now given up to the local authorities to be destroyed." There is no necessity to go, just now, into any account of these false deeds—these little unfortunate things that seem to have occurred in connection with this property—people selling the property who had no right to it, and so on. It resulted in a good deal of trouble, and finally in this agreement of 1866, and there the matter stands. There are now these contiguous pieces of property, forming in fact one piece, partly held under the lease of 1866 and partly under that of 1867, which are still in the defendant's occupation.

I am now coming to the point as to how far your Lordship will be guided in the decision of this case by English law, how far it is possible to introduce English law into the dealings between Englishmen and Chinese with reference to a piece of land in China. According to English law all leases are subject to be construed according to the custom of the country where the premises are situated. The court construes the terms according to the custom of the country; and also the law of the land, as differing from custom, where it can differ in a matter of this kind, would be imported into it where necessary.—The learned counsel quoted the sections of the Order in Council bearing upon the case and went on to say that the English law of landlord and tenant, although certainly very peculiar in some ways, would not, he thought, be found to differ very much from the customs in force in China with reference to leases from year to year. He thought his Lordship would find great similarity between the notions of English people and Chinese with regard to the letting of houses. Of course, when they came to the letting of land for agricultural purposes, that was quite a different matter, but he did not think there would be much confusion of authorities between the customs and laws of the two countries. Whether the words found in this document had ever been found in any English case he did not know; he had been unable to find any such decision himself, but there were a good many cases, some old and some new, which had been decided in England upon documents where there had been an agreement "not to give notice to quit" without any term of years fixed, with no determinate term reserved in the agreement. Where the agreement was that there should be no notice to quit it had been held in the Common Law Courts, although it was not precisely the same in equity in some cases, that these very words were repugnant to the provisions of such a lease. Now treating the document of 1867 for a moment as it stood, looking at it by the light of English law, he presumed that, without extraordinary evidence of some kind, it stood as a lease for an indeterminate period. He cited passages from Woodfall's Law of Landlord and Tenant and the cases of King's Leasehold Estates reported in 16 Law Reports Equity, and Holmes and Day, reported in 8 Irish Reports, C.L., 235 C.P. In this case, he went on to say, the title of the lessors was certainly not for a term of years. Nothing could be more indeterminate, vaguer, or looser in any way than the title of the directors who signed the document dated August, 1867, on behalf of themselves and other directors. Nothing, he thought, could be clearer from the wording of the agreement itself than that what was meant was that the agreement should be an agreement from three months to three months, or, as that was scarcely known to our law, a tenancy from year to year. Therefore, if the words at the end of the document that they should not let the place to any one else were equivalent to an agreement not to give a notice to quit they wou d be repugnant to what was the real meaning between the parties. According to the law of England a lease without any determinate period mentioned in it, which could not be determined by a reference to any contingent event, or any event outside which could be introduced into the document by verbal testimony, was, he apprehended, upon the face of the document itself, a mere tenancy at will. If ever there was a case in which a lease, according to English law, was void for uncertainty, he put it that this was one. As the tenants had entered under a void lease, and they had paid, and the plaintiffs had accepted rent, the title was one of tenancy from year to year, determinable by a three months' notice to quit; by a written notice to quit according to English law, according to Chinese law by the non-acceptance of rent. Rent had been refused by the plaintiffs, but they were not suing so much for ejectment as for a declaration of their rights. Whether they would proceed by any means of ejectment was a matter for after consideration. There was also another aspect of the case, which was that if his Lordship should decide the lease should exist the plaintiffs would ask the decree of the court as to the defendant's right to build on the piece of ground over which he had such right. The learned counsel concluded by pointing out on the plan the different pieces of ground in dispute.

The court then ajourned until the following day.

(SECOND DAY,) May 1st.

Mr. Hayllar now proceeded to call evidence for the plaintiffs.

Mr. Lai Sun, of Shanghai, acted as interpreter in the mandarin dialect.

Ting Kia Wai, ex Prefect of Foochow, was the first witness. He said—I am an officer at Peking, in the service of the Emperor of China. I held office as Prefect for three years at Foochow, and previous to that I had held offices of various grades in the Fuhkien province. I came here when I was twenty-six years old and I am now sixty-three. I have been District Magistrate, sub-Prefect, and Prefect in this province. The administration of justice in civil matters came within my functions in all those offices. (Original agreement of rent in 1867 shown to witness and identified by him.) Mr. Sinclair sent the document to us and we sealed it. It was sent first by Mr. Sinclair to the Board of Trade, of which at that time I was the president. I examined it and found it was in form and then I sent it to the Haukwan Magistrate. After the Magistrate had seen it was in form he sealed it. It was then sent back through the Board of Trade to Consul Sinclair.

Mr. Hayllar asked if the words translated "If not owe rent directors cannot let to anyone else" were a common form in Chinese leases.

Mr. Hannen objected to the question, on the ground that it was put with the object of proving a custom the existence of which was not alleged in the petition and which the plaintiffs could not now set up.

Mr. Hayllar contended that under the rules of the court the evidence could not be set out in the petition nor any argument of law. He referred to Taylor on Evidence to show that testimony to show the meaning of obscure documents was admissible. The document here was in a foreign language and had a technical meaning and could not be interpreted by the court without evidence.

His Lordship overruled the objection, holding that the setting out of the document involved its interpretation.

Evidence continued—The words pointed out to me are a common form in leases for no definite period. If the agreement were for a lease in perpetuity it would be so expressed. I have seen many leases of this kind.

Mr. Hayllar asked what the term would be in a lease in perpetuity.

Mr. Hannen objected to this question on the ground that it was interpreting a document in which there was no ambiguity unless Mr. Hayllar were allowed to bring it in by setting up custom. The document said that as long as the defendant paid rent he was to have the use of the property. There was no ambiguity about that, and if foreign law were to be imported into the matter foreign law was a fact which ought to have been set out in the petition.

After argument, the question was allowed.

Evidence continued—In a perpetual lease, instead of the clause providing the land shall not be let to anyone else you would have the words "yung yuen," meaning in perpetuity.

Mr. Hayllar—What, according to the custom of Foochow, is the meaning attached to the words which have been translated "If the rent does not get into arrears the place cannot be let to any one else."

His Lordship said this was the question the Court had to determine, and he was afraid he could not allow it to be put to the witness.

Mr. Hayllar argued that the words were in a foreign language, and that the Court ought to know the meaning they conveyed to the mind of persons using that language. An English proverb translated into a foreign language without its meaning would be incomprehensible. The custom of China could not be excluded in the interpretation of this document.

His Lordship said he did not intend to exclude it, but he thought the document could not be put into the hands of the witness to interpret.

Mr. Hayllar referred to the case of the Duchesse de Sauré v. Phillips, cited in Taylor on Evidence, as governing the case, the ruling there being that in respect of foreign documents the Court ought to get first a translation, second, an explanation of any terms of art it contained and, thirdly, evidence of the foreign law applicable to it. H put these words as a term of art. He also referred to Addison as an authority in support of his contention.

Mr. Hannen objected to the question on the ground that the interpretation intended to be put upon the document ought to have been set out; also that the law of the country ought to be proved generally, if at all, not that the document should be put into the hands of the witness to interpret.

Mr. Hayllar said he had not done that; he simply asked the meaning of a term of art contained in the document. This was necessary in every foreign document. He also put it on another ground, that of custom, which was imported into every lease.

His Lordship suggested that the question might be put in a different form, for instance, "in an annual lease in Foochow what would be the term used?"

Mr. Hayllar put the question in this form.

Mr. Hannen objected to this question on the same grounds as before; he also argued that the term was not one of art.

Mr. Hayllar said he would put the question in the form in which it was given in the case he had cited—what is the law of China applicable to the instrument?

Mr. Hannen said he had no objection to that question except upon his former grounds.

The witness was then asked what the law applicable to the document was. He said—I would first have to know the grounds on which the parties sued, whether on account of the rent falling into arrear or the lessors wishing the lessee to leave. If the rent were owing, the landlord could resume and take back his house. If no rent were owing the lessors could not let to anyone else, but if the landlord wished to have the house for himself then the tenant must give it up to the landlord, who generally gives a month or two's notice. If the tenant has been in the house a long time it is at the option of the landlord to charge the rent for that time or let the tenant occupy free. I have had to decide many questions arising on similar documents. Under an agreement of this kind the tenant would not be allowed to erect any buildings upon the land leased, nor would he be allowed to alter materially the buildings leased to him. A lease with the terms "yung yuen" in it is granted on payment of a lump sum in the first instance and no rent is paid. I know the Taou Shan Kwan property, to which this document refers. It is public, or Government, property, and there are directors to manage it. It belongs to the Emperor. The temples were built by public subscription. The land belongs to the Government and the buildings to the public of the City of Foochow. (Letter from Hr. Hewlett, to the witness, as Prefect, dated 10th day of the 6th moon of the 4th year of Tung Chi (1865), and another dated the 15th day of the 10th moon of the same year, put into witness's hands and identified by him.) The second letter was to ask me to go myself and see about the erection of the wall about five or six o'clock on the evening of that day. As I had some business on hand I deferred the visit for three days and then went. The place I went to inspect was where the north wall now is. At that time there was only a bamboo fence there. Mr. Hewlett told me they wanted to borrow that piece of land to build a wall there to prevent nuisances. At that time I saw no wall to the north and west enclosing the Bird's Tongue Bridge. I only saw a bamboo fence twenty or thirty feet long. I was not Prefect when the wall was built and I know nothing about it. I left Foochow in 1876. The dispatch now shown to me was addressed to me by Consul Carroll, and is dated 10th year of Tung Chi, 4th moon, 1st day (5th May, 1866).

Cross-examined by Mr. Hannen—I did go myself to inspect the premises before the erection of the wall which has been mentioned. I went in private dress. I sent a deputy to visit the place officially. I myself had no conversation with Mr. Wolfe or any of the missionaries on the occasion of my visit. The substance of the request was that a wall might be built to keep out beggars. There was a path along the north-east side. The permission I gave was to erect a low wall at the north, but there was nothing said about a gate to prevent beggars getting in by this path. Between the wall and the mission house the ground was not very steep. I have seen leases between Chinese exactly like the one of 1867. Leases between Chinese are always signed by the landlord as well as the tenant. Generally two copies are made amongst Chinese, but for foreigners three are made. It is not the custom among Chinese for the lease to be a single document handed by the tenant to the landlord. In Foochow there are some leases that omit those words about not letting to any other person. In such leases as those it is the general custom that three months' notice is given by the landlord of his intention to eject the tenant. It is not the general custom to let the tenant occupy the house for these three months free of rent, but if the tenant has occupied the house a long time the landlord may let him off payment of rent for a month or two. If a house is burnt d wn and the landlord does not care about rebuilding it himself the tenant must obtain the permission of the landlord before he can do so, and then they can make an agreement as to how long the tenant shall occupy it before giving i up to the landlord. There is no such custom as that of the tenant rebuilding the house without coming to an agreement first. I never heard of a lease containing the words "yung yuen" made between Chinese before foreigners arrived here.

Re-examined by Mr. Hayllar—The words "yung yuen" were invented for transactions with foreigners, because the Chinese would not write the words "to sell," and therefore substituted the term "perpetual lease." The transaction is just the same as a sale between Chinese, only a different term is used. Among Chinese the burning down of a house in itself puts an end to the contract under an agreement of rent from year to year or from month to month if the house is burnt down accidentally, but if through the negligence of the tenant he must rebuild it. The name of the deputy I sent to report about the wall was Fuh. He made an official report about it. The document produced is the report. It is dated the 28th day of the 9th month of the 4th year of Tung Chi.

By his Lordship—I have seen a very large number of leases between Chinese and foreigners, several tens, but none for property within the city except the one in question. The property the other leases I have seen applied to was outside the city. I have seen more perpetual leases than leases for a term. I don't think I have seen any leases for a term of years outside the city between Chinese and foreigners. The law and custom with reference to leases is the same inside and outside the city. There is no difference throughout the province, but each province has its own customs.

Ching Che Yeo, the present Haukwan District Magistrate, said—I am a civil officer in the service of the Emperor of China. There are two district magistrates in the city of Foochow, the Min and Haukwan. Part of my duties consists of the administration of justice, and also putting my official seal on leases between Chinese and foreigners and Chinese themselves. I am aware of the laws and customs of this province as regards leases, and it falls within my duties to adjudicate upon such documents. The document produced (the agreement of rent of 18:7) was recorded in my yamên and I saw it when I entered into office. I have seen it since.

Mr. Hannen took the same general objection to the evidence of this witness as to the law of China applicable to the document in question as he took to the evidence of the last witness.

Evidence continued—As regards this instrument, it is a temporary lease and not a perpetual one, and if the landlord wishes to have the property back and to resume the place he can do so under this agreement. Under the words translated in the petition "the rent to be paid quarterly in advance" it is at the option of the landlord to refuse the rent. If the landlord refuses the rent it is equivalent to a notice to quit. According to law the tenant should go at once, but he is generally allowed about half-a-month to find another house, it being at the option of the landlord to allow him to remain for this period free of rent or not. If the parties came to the magistrate about it, the magistrate would say the tenant must go. The same law applies to cases where the rent is payable every three months; the landlord might allow the tenant any time he thought proper to clear out according to the friendship between them. Under this agreement the landlord can't let to any one else. There is a distinction recognised by Chinese law between the landlord resuming for himself and letting to other people. In dealings in land between foreigners and Chinese in Foochow it is the custom for the Haukwan Magistrate to affix his seal after the Consul has affixed his.

By Mr. Hannen—The Magistrate does not affix his seal to agreements for rent between Chinese, except when there is a sale. The law of China is that a temporary lease requires no stamp, but a sale does. A lease to foreigners containing the words "yung yuen" is about the same as a sale between Chinese. I have seen leases like this between Chinese; such documents are almost all alike. It is not the custom for the document which defines the tenancy to be signed by the landlord. This one is signed by the people who purport to be the landlords; that is because the tenants are foreigners. The wording of the document is the same as the usual form of lease between Chinese, but the signing is different. I have never known such a document when between Chinese to be made in triplicate. The usual custom is that one document is made out, signed by the tenant, and handed to the landlord. The words in this document "if the rent does not get into arrears the place cannot be let to any one else" are not generally omitted in Chinese leases but sometimes they are. There are more leases in Foochow with the characters in than without. I judge this from the knowledge I have obtained by people suing each other Under a lease from which the words in question are absent, if the landlord wishes to eject the tenant, according to the law the tenant ought to go out at once. There is no law that he shall live in the house for a certain time rent free; the people make their own arrangements as to that.

Mr. Hayllar did not re-examine this witness.

The Court adjourned until the following day.

(THIRD DAY, May 2nd.)

Evidence for the plaintiffs was continued.

Loo King Fah, one of the plaintiffs, said—I am a director of one of the associations connected with the Taou Shan Kwan Temple, the "Show Shing Shea," the object of which is to show respect for written papers. It is a voluntary association of certain people in the city. A person becomes a member by election by the other members and the payment of subscription. He is elected for no definite period and can leave the association when he likes. The subscription is a monthly one, and if a person fails to pay he ceases to be a member. The association is managed by directors, sometimes two and sometimes three in number, elected by the general body of members. They are elected for an indefinite period. I was elected in 1864 and have served ever since. The Taou Shan Kwan premises are public property. The records of the temple show that the land originally belonged to a man called Sun Chui Chang, who was a literary examiner in the Chekiang province, about the end of the Ming dynasty. On the left hand side of the Taou Shan Kwan there was a rock with the inscription "Son of the Ming dynasty studied here." This rock was removed in 871 by Mr. Wolfe when he built a foreign house. At the beginning of the present dynasty the descendants of Sun Chui Chang gave the land to the public of the city to build temples upon. Money was raised by public subscription in the city of Foochow and temples were built. The buildings are now kept in repair by voluntary subscriptions. The temple has no money of its own apart from these subscriptions. There are thirteen associations connected with the temple now. In 1866 and 1867 there were only nine. The names of some of the present associations are:—the Hsin-i-Shea, the object of which is to supply incense; the Hsiang Tung Shea for supplying incense and lamps; the Kwan Shea, for supplying fresh flowers; and the Heng Shea, for supplying oil for the lamps kept burning before the idols. All the associations have kindred objects, but are in no way connected with each other. When the temple requires repairs the directors of the associations collect the subscriptions, and combine together for this purpose. A Taouist priest conducts the services of the temple, and is elected for that purpose by the directors of the associations generally. The directors have the power of dismissing him. He has no regular salary, but each association contributes some rice to him, and when worshippers go to the temple he gives them some tea, and they cumshaw him money in return; this is called tea money. The temple is open at all times, night and day, and is one which is much frequented. The associations in return for their services to the temple have the use of apartments in the temple, and each association meets five or six times a year. The object of the meetings is to celebrate the idols' birth days. They take place in the first, second, fifth, eighth, and ninth moons of each year. They have services which take the form of theatrical performances, the burning of incense, and the lighting of lamps. These services are public. Besides these there are feasts at which only the subscribers are present. There is a small temple at Taou Shan Kwan called the Blind Man's Temple, where the blind men of the city meet for their religious services and feasts. On two days in the year large numbers of people assemble on the Taou Shan Kwan grounds. These are the 14th day of the 8th and 14th day of the 9th moon. At the south-west corner of the grounds is a rock called Lee Kung's rock, or Wu Shih, which means black rock, and it is from this the hill derives its name. There is another rock called the Bird's Tongue Bridge. The people attach great significance to these rocks as they are supposed to be the origin of fung shui and to be the dragon's pulse. In 1864, when my connection with the temple as a director commenced, the name of the priest in charge was Chun Yuen Ching. Mr. Wolfe was at this time in occupation of several buildings on the premises and resided in the house which was accidentally burnt down in 1871. About the 12th moon of the 4th year of Tung Chi the document produced was brought to my notice. ($800 lease produced). I heard there was a private contract between the priest and Mr. Wolfe. It was spoken of publicly and I saw it on the 1st moon of the succeeding year in the Taou Shan Kwan. This document had not been made with the sanction of the directors; they knew nothing about it. When the directors of the temple heard of this lease they objected to it. The priest had not the least power to deal with the property in this way, and the directors cancelled the document. In the following year, the fifth year of Tung Chi, the 3rd month, the directors heard that the priest had again made an agreement with Mr. Wolfe ($500 lease produced). I saw the document at the Haukwan Magistrate's yamen, where the priest had been sent to be punished. He was in prison there. The directors never knew about the lease until after it was made, and it was cancelled by the Board of Trade in the same month. I do not know if receipts were given for the rent when it was paid by Mr. Wolfe; that was a matter between Mr. Wolfe and the priest. Up to this time the priest had collected the rent. The document now shown to me ($500 promissory note) is a note of money borrowed purporting to be made by Chun Yuen Ching, dated August 13th, 1866 I have seen this for the first time to-day, but I have heard of it before. The directors had given no authority to Chun Yuen Ching to borrow this money and set the rent off against it; they knew nothing about it. Some of the directors reported to the Board of Trade about the non-payment of rent by Mr. Wolfe. They presented a petition in the usual way to the Board of Trade. The document now shown me is the reply of Mr. Sinclair to the Board of Trade, and the petition is copied in it. It is dated in July, 1867. I see another answer from Mr. Sinclair, dated in August, 1867, embodying another petition on the same subject. I was present when the draft of the agreement of rent with Mr. Wolfe in 1867 was written. The earlier agreements had been made with the priests; this was made with the directors. That was because when it became known there had been some peculiar dealings between the missionaries and the priest, the directors thought they would make an agreement of rent with the missionaries themselves. The draft agreement was drawn by Chow Tao Wen and Lin Yune Chin, two of the directors now deceased. They were the directors who signed the agreement after the draft had been returned by the Consul. It was sent back in triplicate. Chow Tao Wen belonged to the Shan Fun Shea, or association for supplying lamps and incense, and Lin Yune Chin to the association for supplying incense to the room appropriated to the gods wordshipped by the literati. These two directors are both dead. All the directors of the nine associations were present when the agreement was signed. Before foreigners came to China there was never such a thing as the letting of Taouist property to anyone. I am an inhabitant of the city of Foochow and have lived here all my life. I am one of the literati. I produce a map of the temple property, which comes from the records of the temple. The date of the map is about 1838. The property remained in the condition there shown until the year 1850.

By Mr. Hannen—I do not know whether the plan is accurate as to small details. It is accurate as to the enclosing wall as it appears on the plan. The land outside the wall does not belong to the Taou Shan Kwan, but is public ground. I myself saw the draft of the agreement of 1867 written by Chow Tao Wen. The document was no composition of our own, but was written according to the custom of Fuhkien. Some parts of it were copied from documents of a similar kind, viz., agreements of rent, one of which was the lease of 1850. We struck out the words which appear in the lease of 1850 with reference to the option of the lessees. Another of the documents we copied from was the agreement of 1855. There was no other document from which we copied.

Mr. Hannen asked the witness if he and his fellow directors received a notice from Mr. Sinclair requesting them to go and point out the exact encroachments alleged against Mr. Wolfe.

Mr. Hayllar said he admitted such a notice was received and that the plaintiffs, acting under his advice, did not attend, as it was after the petition was filed and was one of the questions to be decided.

Cross-examination continued—There is a blind man's association connected with the temple, which was in existence in 1864. I have myself seen the rock I spoke of in my examination-in-chief and the inscription on it—"Son of the Ming dynasty studied here." The Wu Shih rock is outside the mission premises.

Re-examined by Mr. Hayllar—The building which was burnt down last year is outside the enclosing wall of the Taou Shan Kwan as described in the plan I have produced.

Wang Kan, one of the gentry of Foochow and an elder of the city, said—I am seventy-three years of age and a director of one of the associations connected with the Taou Shan Kwan and have been so for twenty-six years. I belong to the Hung Shea, or association for supplying lamp oil to the temple. The enclosing wall indicated on the plan produced is correctly shown. The land outside that is public ground and not the property of the temple. The house burnt down last year stood outside the enclosing wall.

By Mr. Hannen—The premises continued as shown on the plan up to 1850.

The Court adjourned until the following day.

(FOURTH DAY, 3rd May.)

Evidence for the plaintiffs was continued.

Chun Yuen Ching said—I am a Buddhist priest. I was formerly a Taouist priest, and was at the Taou Shan Kwan. I joined that temple in 1843, and was at that time the junior of three priests. The head priest's name was Hwang Chiao Ming, and that of the second Ling Yung Mow. I remember when foreigners first came to the temple in 1844. An Englishman named Morrison at that time came to reside in the temple. (Points out building on the plan). I remember the year 1850. The senior priest was then Ling Yung Mow. In that year two missionaries named Wung Tung (Welton) and Cha Sing (Jackson) came to reside in the temple. Cha Sing lived on the left hand side of the Taou Shan Kwan in a place called the San Pao Tien and Wung Tung lived at the Wu Ss Tien, a place also on the left hand side. There were idols in these two buildings before the arrival of the missionaries, but they were removed when the premises were let. The buildings were Chinese structures without any upper story. I became the head priest of the temple in 1853. Soon after this I let a place on the right hand side of the temple to Hwan Lee (Fearnley). There was a written agreement The document produced is that agreement. It is in my handwriting.

A question here arose as to the signature to the document, which was not the same as the characters used in the body. Sir Thomas Wade, who was present, explained that most Chinamen, in addition to the characters for their name which appeared in the body of documents, had a private mark which they used as their signature. Prince Kung used a sentence from Confucius for his signature, and no one would know what it meant without his explanation.

Examination continued—The building I let was a one storied one. I have visited the place recently. The three houses I have marked on the map as having been let to the missionaries are now entirely different from what they were before. I saw the alterations being made in the San Pao Tien in 1855. They were being made by a missionary named Smith, who acted on his own authority in the matter; no one gave him permission. The Wu Ss Tien was altered in 1856 or 1857 by Mr. Fearnley, who also acted without permission. The building when it was altered did not cover the same ground as it did originally. The Wu Ss Tien originally faced the east. It was made to face the south and some buildings on the west were altered. The house was removed further towards the east up to the temple wall. (Witness points out on the plan the limits of the land let under the lease of 1855.) The buildings I let in 1855 are not in the same state as they were in when I let them. I don't know when they were altered. I also let a small piece of ground towards the north-west, outside the boundary wall of the temple property. I let that to Mr. Smith in 1861 by verbal agreement. The rent was $1 a month. Formerly there was a door in the enclosing wall of the Taou Shan Kwan and in consequence of people going through that door to go up to an elevated place which overlooked the mission premises Mr. Smith said he wanted the piece of land in question to block up the door. The place was called the Fang Ko Tien. I made some other agreements in reference to the property. It is so long ago that I cannot remember what they were, but I will recognise my handwriting if I see them. I left the Taou Shan Kwan in 1867.

The witness was asked why he left. He appeared considerably affected and looking towards Mr. Wolfe suggested that he should be asked the question.

Evidence continued—I had dealings with Mr. Wolfe in reference to this property. Mr. Wolfe told me in 1865 that he would make a perpetual lease with me so that it would prevent my going for the yearly rent. After a great many consultations between us the lease w s written. The agreement was for $800 and I wrote the lease with my own hand, but Mr. Wolfe gave me the draft to copy from. The document shown to me is not written by myself, but it bears my signature. I thought I copied it out, it is so long ago, but I see it is not so. I don't know who wrote it, but Mr. Wolfe brought it to me for my signature. After I had signed it Mr. Wolfe took it away and said he would himself see about the affixing of the official seal by the mandarins. I did not receive the $800 mentioned in the agreement. Mr. Wolfe told me that if he got the document stamped I would receive the money and that if he did not I was not to receive it. In 1867 there was another agreement. Mr. Wolfe came to consult with me about another perpetual lease for $500. Such an agreement was written. I do not remember who wrote it.

Mr. Hayllar explained that the original of the agreement in question was sent to the Consulate and could not now be found. He proposed to put into the witness's hands a copy made in the yamen, which he would afterwards prove.

Evidence continued—The document produced is an exact copy of the agreement. I never received a cent of the $500 mentioned in it. I was to receive it when the official seal was affixed to it and it never was affixed. On account of this document I was sent to the yamen and kept in prison for four or five days. Mr. Wolfe bailed me out. In the 7th moon of the same year Mr. Wolfe came to me again and wanted to consult about another perpetual lease, but I said I had been imprisoned for four or five days in consequence of the last one and I dare not make another. Mr. Wolfe then told me that he had a plan to suggest. He said we need not make a perpetual lease, but he would lend me the $500 on a promissory note, the interest on which was to be $11 a month, which was the equivalent of the rent. A promissory note was brought to me by Mr. Wolfe and I signed it. (Document shown to witness). The first part, up to the signature, is the document as I signed it, but the rest has been attached.

Mr. Hayllar explained that the appendage was an enclosure from the Consulate which was attached to the note in the yamen.

Evidence continued—I received the $500 mentioned in the note in three instalments after I had signed the note. The first instalment was about $200. I received the last instalment in the 2nd moon of the 6th year of Tung Chi (1867), some day after the 20th. That instalment was

$130 or $140. Mr. Wolfe paid me the money and made a memorandum at the end of the document. The memorandum is not on the document now. After I received the last instalment I heard that people outside had wind of the affair and in my fright I went to Mr. Wolfe to ask his advice as to what I should do. Mr. Wolfe told me I had better go to some other place and hide for a month or two. I acted on Mr. Wolfe's advice and went away at the end of the 2nd moon or beginning of the 3rd moon of the 6th year of Tung Chi. I was afraid to come back and have remained in concealment up to the present.

Cross-examined by Mr. Hannen—It is true that I executed a perpetual lease for the whole of the property to Mr. Wolfe for $800, but it did not come to anything. I had no right to make such a lease. I had no right to execute the lease for $500 either. I have said Mr. Wolfe told me he had a plan. He meant a plan to obtain the same end as a perpetual lease only in a different way. I got the money for myself, not for the services of the temple. Mr. Wolfe suggested this. I had only dealings with Mr. Smith in reference to one piece of ground. I think the characters on the document now shown to me are my signature. Now I see the body of the document I say it is not genuine. Even if I get punished for it I say so. As I read the document, it purports to be a perpetual lease given by me for a small piece of ground outside the temple for $25. The piece of ground I let to Mr. Smith for $12 per annum was over ten feet from east to west and about twelve feet from north to south. The rent of the four-roomed house I let at the south-west corner was $20 per annum. As to the $800 lease I am sure Mr. Wolfe took the document away with him and sent it to the yamen. I do not remember whether there were two copies, of which I kept one. First I sold the property for $800, afterwards for $500. That was Mr. Wolfe's idea. Mr. Wolfe might say the price was tens of thousands of dollars, but he ought to have a conscience before heaven. The price was not $1,500 but $500, and even that was not successful. I only saw the document making the sale for $500 once. The memorandum of the payments on the $500 promissory note was made at the left hand side of the document. Up to 1867 the priest had always collected the rent and made the agreements. I and the other priests knew of the alterations made in the buildings. Before Mr. Fearnley came no alterations had been made outside the buildings. I made some objections to the external alterations made by Mr. Fearnley. I never sold or offered to sell the Blind Man's Temple to Mr. Wolfe.

By Mr. Hayllar—When I spoke to Mr. Fearnley about the alterations he said he was only going to make a few external alterations to keep the sun off. I said nothing more. I never before saw the document purporting to be a perpetual lease of land to Mr. Smith for $12 nor did I ever hear anything about it before to-day.

Siu Chee Chen said—I am the head priest at the Taou Shan Kwan and became so in 1870. I remember the mission house which was burnt down in December of that year. The house which has been built in its place occupies a larger site, It has been extended towards the west. I see marked on the plan the rock on which was the inscription "Son of the Ming dynasty studied here." I knew the rock. As Mr. Mahood wished to extend the house when he was rebuilding it this rock was removed. At the time of the fire the rock burst—I mean about an inch in thickness broke off. Mr. Mahood removed part of the rock when he was rebuilding and on part of it the wall is built. After the fire some of the gentry were worshipping at the temple and hearing the noise of stone cutting they went over with me and remonstrated with Mr. Mahood about cutting that rock. Mr. Mahood said he was rebuilding the house but did not intend to encroach at all. There was an enclosing wall on the north-west. In 1876 that wall was removed and another wall put up further out. This wall was removed. The wall now standing is not on the site of the one which was removed in 1876; it is a little further out.

Cross-examined by Mr. Hannen—The distance of the existing wall from the line of the original wall varies. I cannot say what the greatest distance is. Before the house was burnt down in 1870 there were no buildings extending to the door in the wall. I do not know if there were not outhouses extending almost to the door. (Witness marks on the plan the site occupied by the house burnt down in 1870, and that occupied by the new building). The old house had one storey above the ground floor.

Mr. Hayllar did not re-examine this witness.

Chow Chang Kung, one of the plaintiffs, was called to prove his position as a director of one of the associations connected with the temple.

By Mr. Hannen—I have known the premises for about fifteen years. I can't point out the site occupied by the house burnt down in 1870, but I know the house was a smaller one than the present one. Lin King Ching and Sat Keok Min are directors in the same way as I am. The four plaintiffs mentioned in the petition were appointed by all the directors to represent their interests.

This brought the evidence for the plaintiffs to a close with the exception of the proof of documents to be produced, and the court at its rising adjourned until Monday, the 5th May.

(FIFTH DAY, May 5th.)

Mr. Hayllar now tendered in evidence the documents which had been referred to in the plaintiffs' case.

Ho Aloy was called to prove the translations. He said he was formerly chief interpreter in the Police Court at Hongkong and resigned in 1866. Fe gave formal evidence as to the accuracy of the translations produced.

The agreements of rent of 1850 and 1855 were admitted.

Two despatches of Mr. Consul Hewlitt to the Prefect, and the Prefect's reply thereto, in reference to the building of a wall outside the temple grounds, were objected to by Mr. Hannen, on the ground that the defendant was not bound by the documents, and that they could not be evidence against him. After discussion Mr. Hayllar withdrew the documents, Mr. Hannen admitting the fact that permission to build the wall referred to was applied for and granted.

The perpetual lease for $800, made by the Taouist priest and afterwards cancelled, was objected to by Mr. Hannen on the ground that there was no evidence where it came from or whose it now was. All they knew was that a certain document was laid before the priest, who said it was a document he had seen before; he said Mr. Wolfe brought it to him and took it away again, and it was not shown how it got into other hands.

Mr. Hayllar argued that the document was admissible on the evidence of the priest, who said it was the document he signed. If the defendants said it was forgery they could call proof as to that, and it would be a matter of evidence.

His Lordship ruled that the document was admissible, it being open to Mr. Hannen to contradict it if he was able to do so.

With reference to the perpetual lease for $500 made by the priest and afterwards cancelled, Mr. Hannen objected to the document produced being received in evidence on the ground that it was only a copy and that nothing had been proved as to the loss of the original document entitling his friend to put in a copy.

Mr. Hayllar said he had the clearest proof that the original was sent to the Consul, and he would call evidence to prove that it was not in the consulate now and that in the ordinary course it would most probably have been returned to Mr. Wolfe.

Mr. C. A. Sinclair, H.B.M. Consul at Foochow, gave evidence to the effect stated by the learned counsel.

Mr. Hayllar asked Mr. Hannen if he said the copy was a forgery.

Mr. Hannen said he did not, but there was a mistake in one of the amounts put down.

Mr. Hayllar wished to call his learned friend's attention to the dispatches on the subject. In Mr. Consul Carroll's dispatches it was referred to over and over again as a $500 lease.

Mr. Hannen contended that notice ought to have been given to the defendant to produce the original.

Mr. Hayllar said he was under the impression the document was in the Consulate, and it was not until Saturday he found it was not. He would, however, ask Mr. Wolfe if he had the original.

Mr. Wolfe replied that he had not.

The document was then admitted in evidence.

The promissory note for $500 given by the priest was admitted, and the agreement of rent of 1867.

A dispatch from Mr. Consul Carroll to the Prefect was tendered in evidence by Mr. Hayllar.

Mr. Hannen objected to the reception of the document on the ground that the defendant was not a party to it and that it therefore i ; no way bound him.

Mr. Hayllar said the document showed that the whole matter had been stirred up and that the Consul gave an opinion on it, clearly acting in an official character. He was not acting merely in a *quasi* official character as the Consul sometimes did, and as Mr. Hewlitt did in reference to the wall. Mr. Carroll said—" After careful consideration of this matter, I see no reason why the premises occupied by Mr. Wolfe should not be still rented at a yearly tenancy, though their being rented for a perpetual term is inconsistent with reason."

His Lordship asked if Mr. Wolfe was to be bound by all documents written by the Consul.

Mr. Hayllar—By no means, but he is bound by this.

His Lordship—How do you show the privity?

Mr. Hayllar said that was immaterial. The Consul was acting under the powers conferred upon him by treaty to act as a court of conciliation. He was acting in an official capacity, and this despatch was an official act in reference to this case which subsequently had a most important bearing upon it. He gave a decision that after all that had been done, after the perpetual lease had been refused, they should go on at a yearly rental. The Chinese acted on Mr. Carroll's suggestion; the official interference which came at that time they yielded to.

The Judge asked if Mr. Hayllar contended the court was to be bound by what Mr. Carroll had done.

Mr. Hayllar said he did not contend the court was bound by it, but the plaintiffs considered they were.

Mr. Hannen—And we are bound by this letter written behind our backs?

Mr. Hayllar—He was your protector. not ours. He was to do the best he could for you, not for us; and, having taken into consideration the whole case he makes a suggestion.

His Lordship—Did the defendants act upon that suggestion?

Mr. Hayllar—Yes. In point of fact we went on upon the old lease until December, 1867. Official acts in cases of this kind were not to be lightly set aside, because they entered into the pith and marrow of the whole thing. We say this is the proper way of communicating with us. Where the impropriety came in was when they treated with our priest. This we regard as a completely official act. It is the duty of the Consul to interfere in all these cases.

His Lordship—And to bind the parties?

Mr. Hayllar—Yes, when the act is accepted. If Mr. Wolfe had not remained, the Consul's act would not have bound him. Mr. Wolfe set the thing in motion. He got the deed from the priest, he sent it then to the Consul. He is the person who is acting, not we. The Consul sends it to the authorities, all on behalf of his interest. The authorities send it back and then the consul returns it to Mr. Wolfe and decides "There is no reason why the premises occupied by Mr. Wolfe should not be still rented at a yearly tenancy, though their being rented for a perpetual term is inconsistent with reason." That was a judicial act with reference to the lease of 1866 and the Consul's resolution upon it. If it is anything, it is a judicial act as clearly as a judicial act can be, that is to say, official. The learned counsel then referred to the 17th section of the Treaty of Tientsin, providing that the Consul shall hear and settle in a friendly manner complaints against Chinese by British subjects and equally shall hear and endeavour to settle complaints by Chinese against British subjects. Here the Chinese had very great reason to complain of a British subject, and it was clearly under the treaty that Mr. Carroll had been acting.

His Lordship—This is negotiating a lease. He tried to get a good thing and did not succeed.

Mr. Hayllar—No; but how did he not succeed? by our making complaint against a British subject. As soon as this lease was brought before us we made very considerable complaint, and Mr. Carroll then acted under article 17 of the Treaty. Ninety-nine hundredths of the business between Chinese and foreigners is managed in that way. Fortunately it generally stops short of litigation, and it is the business of the Consul to make it stop short if he can. In this case he did.

His Lordship—You want to show that, having regard to that letter, you cannot have intended to confer anything more than an annual lease?

Mr. Hayllar—Exactly. The question was then stirred up and we did what we were asked to do.

His Lordship said he could not admit the document. He thought the defendant could not be held to be bound in any way by this document. It was a document written by Mr. Carroll to the Prefect, and was not brought to the cognisance of the defendant.

Mr. Hayllar then tendered three other documents—a dispatch from Mr. Consul Sinclair to the Board of Trade, one from the Board of Trade to Mr. Sinclair, and another from Mr. Sinclair to the Board of Trade—which he contended were admissible as being the negotiations which led to the lease of 1867. The learned counsel read the dispatches, which were as follow:—

Sinclair, H.B.M. Consul for Foochow, to Chang Taotai and others, the Committee of the Board of Foreign Trade.

Sirs,—In your despatch which reached me on the 20th day of the present month, a joint petition of Chao Tao Wen and others, directors of the Tao Shan Kwan temple, is quoted which represents as follows:—

"That the premises in the Tao Shan Kwan temple were let to the foreigners at an annual rent of $172, payable quarterly, which rent used to be handed over to the Taouist priest at the temple named Chun Yuen Ching, and his student Sit Min Yung, to defray the expenses of the services therein; that since Chun Yuen Ching absconded in the third month of the present year the petitioners have employed another Taouist priest named Tsai Min Ho to take charge of the services above-mentioned, and, upon the Haukwan District Magistrate submitting their petition to his superior officers, an official dispatch was forwarded (to the Consul) requesting that the missionary Wolfe should pay to Tsai Min Ho the rent for the summer quarter and all rents thereafter becoming due, that the same might be appropriated for defraying the expenses of the services in the temple; that the petitioners have learnt with extreme surprise that the missionary Wolfe has made a reply to the effect that the rent for the summer quarter had already been collected by Chun Yuen Ching and Sit Min Yung, and also, on the 4th day of the 7th moon in the preceding year borrowed of him $500, agreeing that the interest accruing therefrom might be set off against the rent; that the petitioners would call their Excellencies' attention to the fact of Chun Yuen Ching and Sit Min Yung having but recently in the 5th month last year improperly and surreptitiously sold to the missionary Wolfe worshipping rooms and land inside and outside the Tao Shan Kwan temple respectively for building purposes, whom they (the petitioners) had seized and brought for examination before the late Haukwan District Magistrate. To him they (Chun Yuen Ching and Sit Min Yung) confessed their guilt and were imprisoned; that subsequently the Consul in his dispatch considering that as the property at the Tao Shan Kwan temple could not be leased for a perpetual term, owing to the temple having been built by the gentry and people, gave up the lease. Accordingly for the original premises occupied by him (Wolfe) he has continued to pay annual rent as of old, and Ting, the late Prefect, having directed the District Magistrate to take a lenient view of the case, the priest Chun Yuen Ching and his student were released on bail, and consequently a proclamation prohibiting surreptitious sale (of the property) was issued. That it would be impossible for one to believe that the missionary Wolfe would have agreed to give the priest that loan so shortly after the disposal of the case above-mentioned, much less would one believe it as the note of money loan does not bear the seal of the Tepao nor the signature of a guarantor. It is quite evident that Wolfe, taking advantage of the absence of the priest and none to come forward to contradict has himself made the note with a view to evade the payments of rent. That supposing the loan was a fact, it would be no more than a matter of private dealing between the two parties. Separate proceedings ought therefore to be taken for recovery of the money, and the rent by no means can be set off against the interest, which, if allowed, would interfere seriously with the services in the temple. That the petitioners therefore pray that a communication be sent with a request that the missionary Wolfe should immediately pay the rent for the summer quarter of the present year and all the rents hereafter due for each quarter to them (Chao Tao Wen and others of the gentry) that the same may be transmitted to the newly appointed priest for defraying the expenses of the services in the temple, and that proceedings for satisfying Wolfe's claim should be treated separately in order that the rent may not be appropriated, &c."

With reference to the case in question you state that the Haukwan District Magistrate has made a report of the same which has been communicated to me through the Board of Trade and to which I have made a reply. You further state that while you have given instructions to the Magistrate of Fu Ching to secretly arrest the priest for investigation and declared an answer to the petition of the Directors, you would also request me to immediately order that the missionary Wolfe should make quarterly payments of the rent commencing from the summer quarter of the present year, and to answer yours on the same; and you further state that as to the case of money loan owed by Chun Yuen Ching it should stand over till Chun Yuen Ching shall have been arrested and brought to the city by the Fu Ching Magistrate, in order that no complication may arise and friendly relations may be maintained, etc., etc. The above I have duly noted, and I beg to state that on receipt of your former dispatch I had on the 3rd day of last month looked up all the leases of past years and found that the total amount of rent per annum is in reality $132, and, having communicated the same in my last reply to yours, I also pointed out that very likely the Directors through a mistake add to their reckoning the amount of rent which a British merchant who has returned to his native country, used to pay, which would exactly make up the sum of $172. Now the missionary John Wolfe has, in pursuance of my order payed $33, being rent due for the summer quarter commencing on the 1st April and ending on the 30th of June this year, corresponding to the Chinese 27th of the 3rd month to the 29th of the 5th month. The same amount I herewith send you with this reply, begging that you will instruct Chao Tao Wen, the Director, to immediately hand it over to the newly appointed priest for the purpose of defraying the expenses of the services in the temple. The priest may personally call on the missionary Wolfe and collect from him rent due for the autumn quarter commencing on the 30th day of the 5th Chinese moon and ending on the 3rd day of the 9th moon, corresponding to 1st July to 30th September, and from henceforth the said missionary shall pay rent according to the English calendar without giving the trouble of writing correspondence about the same. With regard to the leases which I forwarded to you for examination on the 3rd of last month, I beg that you will first return them to me. As to the note of the loan of Chun Yuen Ching and the order, I hope you will give strict orders to the runners of the Prefect's Yamên to co-operate with those of the Fu Ching Magistrate that they may in earnest prosecute the search and apprehension of the absconding priest, Chun Yuen Ching, and his student, etc., etc.

[L.S.] CHAS. A. SINCLAIR.

Tung Chi. 6th year, 6th moon, 25th day.

Chang Taotai and others, Committee of the Board of Foreign Trade, to Sinclair, the British Consul for Foochow.

SIR,—We have received through you the sum of $33, handed over to you by Missionary Wolfe and being payment of the rent of the Tao Shan Kwan premises due for the summer quarter ending the 29th day of the 5th moon of the present year. You request that Chao Tao Wen, the director of the temple should at once deliver the money to the newly appointed priest that he may apply it to the services therein; that the priest may hereafter personally call and collect the rent from Mr. Wolfe with a view of saving the trouble of writing dispatches; that the lease or leases which you have the other day sent us be returned to you; and that we should immediately order the search and arrest of the priest Chun Yuen Ching, who had fraudulently obtained the loan, etc., etc.

We have, as requested, instructed Chow Tao Wen and other of the directors who have accordingly given a receipt for and without delay handed over to the priest Tsai Min Ho the money they received from us. They represented that as the priests in charge are generally employed at their pleasure and occasionally dismissed for misconduct, a recurrence of the evil may happen if the priest in charge should be allowed to personally collect the rent. They consequently pray us to communicate to you a request that the quarterly rent paid by Mr. Wolfe be sent to the Board through you and handed over to them for transmission to the priest in charge for defraying the expenses of the services in the temple. They further pray that the old lease or leases be cancelled and that Mr. Wolfe be ordered to hire of them the premises and make in lieu an agreement of rent which is to be sealed by both (the Consul and Magistrate) and to be kept by the respective parties. The rent we mentioned has heretofore been paid to the priest personally by the said Missionary, but as the private loan case of the priest Chun Yuen Ching has happened, the usual mode of payment should change and cannot be continued. That similar evils may not recur, we therefore grant the prayer above mentioned and communicate the same for your consideration.

While we have replied to the petition of the directors and filed the receipt given for the summer quarter rent, same having been handed over to the priest Tsai Min Ho for defraying the expenses of the services by the directors, we now beg to send you this reply with a copy of the draft of the agreement of rent, begging that you will order Mr. Wolfe to make this day, according to the draft, an agreement of rent in triplicate in lieu of the one or ones formerly made, that the same may be brought to us for transmission to the District Magistrate, who shall impress his seal thereon, and that the same may be returned to you through the Board, with the exception of the one that should be retained at the Magistracy. And with a view of putting a stop to such evils we further beg that you will send regularly quarterly payment of rent that it may through the directors be handed over to the priest for defraying the expenses of the services in the temple, etc., etc.

Tung Chi, 6th year, 7th month, 9th day (August 1878.)

Sinclair, British Consul for Foochow, to Chang Tao-tai; Wen, the Prefect of Foochow; Li, the Prefect of Jing-Ping-foo, Committee of the Board of Trade.

SIRS,—The British Missionary John Wolfe having handed over to me an agreement of rent in triplicate for the Tao Shan Kwan premises in exchange (of the old one), with a request that the three documents be sent to the authorities to be stamped with an official seal, in accordance with the established rules, I herewith forward them on to you begging that you will order the District Magistrate to impress his seal thereon and return them to me after they have been so sealed with the exception of one that is to be left with and kept (at the Magistracy). The old agreement of rent you are hereby also requested to return to me in order that it may be cancelled.

With regard to the late priests of the temple, Chun Yuen Ching and Sit Min Yung, who have absconded with the $500 which they had borrowed of the said Missionary, it is found, on inquiry that their family house is in Fuh Ching and that they have often been seen frequenting the Foochow city and may easily be apprehended. You are therefore earnestly requested to issue strict orders to the runners of the Prefect's Yamen and those of the Fu Ching for their immediate arrest and appearance in court, etc., etc.

The enclosures are as follow:—

Three documents, agreement of rent in triplicate made by John Wolfe in exchange of the old ones.

The draft of the above mentioned agreement of rent originally sent to me.

Tung Chi, 6th year, 7th month, 18th day (August 1867.)

After some discussion as to the admissibility of these documents, his Lordship asked Mr. Hayllar if he insisted upon them.

Mr. Hayllar—Well, my Lord, we would offer official documents in such a case as this rather than in others. They are the evidence of our good faith in the matter. I don't know with what object my learned friend keeps them out, but that is neither here nor there. As your Lordship sees, they don't carry the verbal testimony much further, but there they are, the official records of these acts which took place a good many years ago.

His Lordship—The question is whether you can bring these letters home to Mr. Wolfe.

Mr. Hayllar—I dare say by and by I shall have the opportunity of examining Mr. Wolfe and seeing how they can be brought home to him. At present I tender them as official records to prove our good faith—more for that than anything else. Perhaps in another kind of case I should not have thought it necessary, but in such a case as this, where there is so much in dispute which takes an explosive character it seemed necessary to me that I should tender this evidence. If my learned friend keeps them out that is on his own responsibility. I don't wish to snatch anything, and if your Lordship thinks they are not admissible I should be the last person to press it, but I consider it my duty to tender them and to argue the point.

His Lordship—If Mr. Hannen objects I don't think they are fairly admissible; I am speaking now of the first one.

Mr. Hannen—I do object.

His Lordship—Then the second one?

Mr. Hayllar—I don't think the documents carry the case further than my verbal testimony, but the question would naturally be asked on the other side, why, as these things were conducted through official dispatches, are the despatches not here? I tender them and I don't withdraw them.

The second of the dispatches was disallowed and the third admitted.

Mr. Hannen, not being prepared to cross-examine Mr. Ho Aloy on the accuracy of his translations at this stage,

Mr. Hayllar said he would retender the witness for cross-examination at any time if his friend wished it. There was one question with reference to the non-acceptance of rent as to which he ought to have asked one of the directors. He asked to be allowed to recall him and said that would close his case.

Mr. Hannen objected to the evidence on the formal ground that the allegation was not made in the petition.

Mr. Hayllar asked permission to amend the petition on this point, which was granted, and a paragraph was accordingly added making the necessary allegation.

Loo King Fah, recalled, proved that rent had been refused since June last, $132 in all.

By Mr. Hannen—The rent was received thro gh the Board of Trade, and when it was refused notice was given to the Board.

Mr. Sinclair, recalled, said he had been informed that the rent had been refused.

By Mr. Hannen—He was not quite certain whether he communicated the fact of the refusal of the rent to Mr. Wolfe.

This closed the case for the plaintiffs.

Mr. Hannen asked that the petition be dismissed on the ground that no case had been made out. He supported his application on purely technical grounds, the principal point taken being that no declaration of rights could be made except upon application for specific relief.

After argument this point was overruled.

As the court was rising, his Lordship recommended a compromise, and the learned counsel were called into the Judge's private room. The result of the conference had not transpired when our report left.

(SIXTH DAY, May 7th.)

The negotiations for a settlement of the case having fallen through, Mr. Hannen now opened the case for the defence.

The settlement preposed by the Chief Justice was that the missionaries should remove their schools and college from Wu Shih Shan into premises to be provided by the Chinese Government within the settlement, and should be allowed to reside with their families in the buildings now occupied by them at the Taou Shan Kwan. The following letters passed between Counsel on the subject:—

FOOCHOW, May 6th, 1879.

MY DEAR HANNEN,—I understood from you this morning that you were empowered to treat with us in reference to the Judge's proposed compromise of the Wu Shih Shan case only on the basis of being granted a lease for a long term of years of the Mission premises. After a long and patient consideration of the subject with me, my clients must decline to treat with yours on that basis, as they find the condition one which it is quite impossible to fulfil. The Chief-Justice's scheme of conciliation must be therefore regarded as having fallen through.

I have, however, laid before the Authorities the alternative plan proposed by the Minister, and after consulting the map of the city with Sir Thomas Wade and myself they have, in deference to my wishes and in order to promote peace, decided to offer you once more the only one of the five or six sites in the city previously offered to you which they regard as entirely unobjectionable for the erection of both schools and residence, viz., the one at the South-west corner of the city. Sir Thomas Wade expressed to-day his opinion that he would not hesitate to put a consulate there, and the Taotais assure me that it is regarded by the Chinese as being as healthy as any other part of the city. I have personally used much exertion to obtain this offer for your clients, and I trust they will take it into their earnest consideration.

Failing its acceptance there is no alternative before us but to proceed with the trial.—I am, my dear Hannen, very truly yours,

THOMAS C. HAYLLAR.

May 6th, 1879.

MY DEAR HAYLLAR,—I have laid before my clients your letter to me of this date and I enclose their reply. I have communicated to the Chief-Justice the result of our negotiations and have asked him not to sit until 2 p.m. to-morrow.—Yours truly,

NICHOLAS J. HANNEN.

T. C. Hayllar, Esq., Q C.

(Enclosure.)

May 6th, 1879.

DEAR MR. HANNEN,—With reference to the proposal contained in Mr. Hayllar's letter to you to-day, offering us a piece of property to the south-west of the city, a great part of which is at present covered with water, as a compromise and settlement of the questions now at issue between us, after careful consideration we are compelled, on account of the unsuitableness of the situation, and the opinion of Dr. Stewart as to its unhealthiness, to decline accepting it.—Yours very truly,

JOHN R. WOLFE.

Mr. Hannen said—May it please your Lordship it now becomes my duty to open the case for the defence, and I shall endeavour to shorten as much as I can the few remarks I have to make at this stage of the case so that we may get on to the main thing, the evidence, and hereafter, when the opportunity occurs for my recurring to any of the subjects if it is necessary, I can lengthen and emphasise the points I now lay before your Lordship as shortly as I can. Having attended carefully to my learned friend's opening, the case appears to be one which divides itself broadly into four points. The first, and one prominent point which forces itself on my mind, and which I am afraid is also in my client's mind, is the priest's story. It is really a very unfortunate thing that that story, which has really nothing to do with the case, has been imported into it—a story which depends upon the testimony of one man, which in its insinuations is very unpleasant, and which has no legal bearing on this case. However there it is. There is the priest's story and it stands like a thorn in our way. The next chapter in the matter is the alleged encroachments, another very unpleasant thorn, but one which I feel quite confident will, before this case has gone half through the rest of its length, have fallen to the ground. After that comes the question of the parcels, and after that comes the legal effect of the documents which have been laid before the court. I am bound to come to the priest's story first, and I ask your Lordship to consider for a moment the excessive improbability of the whole story. What does it amount to? It amounts to a statement that in the 4th year of Tung Chi my client attempted to seduce this innocent old gentleman into making a sale of the property for a sum of $800; that, having failed in that, he then, about a year afterwards, makes another attempt, but this time, knowing that the directors have refused to sanction the transaction, he thinks it will be made a great deal more easy by his offering $500 instead of $800. Then he winds up with a deep laid scheme which shows he must have known the whole of the law referring to property in China as my learned friend hardly knows it after his long study of this case and the assistance he has been able to obtain from the authorities and the various people connected with it. Now I think that, on the very face of it, shows the story to be so improbable as hardly to need any refutation. On the other hand, what is Mr. Wolfe's version of the story? His account has been set out in his answer, but I may briefly put it before your Lordship. It is simply this—The priest goes first with a proposition, no doubt suggested by my client, who is anxious to get the Blind Man's Temple. It is exceedingly probable, and in fact we have discovered in turning over all sorts of records since this case began, matter which leads us to believe that there was an actual offer to purchase that temple about the time which is indicated in the petition by the $800 lease. Therefore my client's case is that at that time an attempt was made to purchase the temple, that the priest came and said he had obtained the permission of the proper authorities to sell it, and that there that matter ended. It faded away. The proper authorities afterwards would not give their consent, or possibly, it is so long ago it is not easy to remember, but it is possible some one came afterwards and said they could not; but so far as our case is concerned, the fact of there having been a deed for the sale of the temple for $800 is outside our case; we know nothing about it. Then some considerable time after that—in the petition it is laid at a distance of about five months—the priest again goes and says "I have now obtained the permission of the people connected with the temple to sell the whole of the property which you occupy." Upon that my client set to work in the ordinary way, a deed was drawn up, it was shown to the priest, and it was sent to the Consul in the ordinary manner. There was nothing in the least underhand about it. The deeds were sent by the Consul to the authorities in a formal dispatch, and after some time they came back to the Consul with the information that the priest had no authority to sell, and there is an end of the matter. Then my client naturally goes to the priest and asks "How about that $500 paid on account?" He says "I cannot pay it now; I will give you a promissory note for it, and the interest"—I suppose he said in his desire to calm my client in his demand for the return of money paid on account—"I will make the interest on the amount equivalent to the rent, and you shall not be bothered with any payment of rent as long as I am here." The next thing is that the priest absconds, and the way this document gets into the hands of the authorities is by my client sending it to the Consul to forward to the authorities in order to get his money back. Mr. Sinclair sends the reply to my client. My client writes back, "Ought I not to be entitled to set off what is due from the priest to me against the rent?" and Mr. Sinclair writes back to say, "No, you ought not," and then the rent is paid. There was no question of any order; it was simply an inquiry on the one part and an answer on the other. That is the whole explanation of the transaction which has been made so much of, which has been put forward in such an exceedingly unpleasant manner. Now, with regard to the statements the priest makes, the inferences which are to be drawn from them and which are really on the surface, although my learned friend, with his well known tact and ability, has avoided actually saying from his own mouth what they are—but the insinuations which are contained in those statements are utterly false, and not only false, but absurd. To imagine my client could at that time have known so much of the law of China as to believe that by in some way contriving not to pay the rent he would be able to lay some claim to the premises is more than any reasonable person could do. The danger of the priest's story lies in the mixture of truth and falsehood it contains. There was some kind of negotiation first, there was a second negotiation which had to do with $500, and there was a promissory note. That has been so contrived by the priest, whose plain interest it is to make out he was an innocent party, led off by my client to do what was wrong, whose plain interest it is to say everything that agrees with the plaintiffs' case—the plaintiffs were the parties who arrested him once, the plaintiffs are the people who will have a right to complain of his conduct if they like, for he has been in hiding, and therefore his most vital interest lies in saying everything he can in favour of the plaintiffs' case and in opposition to mine. Now, seeing what small corroboration there is to the story, I don't think your Lordship will give much consideration to it, but I am bound, until I know your Lordship feels no difficulty on the point, to put forward every one of the considerations which it is necessary to use in order to lay the foundation of my argument that the whole thing should be entirely swept away as beside the question, and if not beside the question, entirely false. Now, with regard to that copy of the $800 deed, it is not accounted for in any way whatever.

Mr. Hayllar—It is the original.

Mr. Hannen—Well, the original, if you like to call it so. The way in which it is accounted for, so far as it goes, is this: the priest says Mr. Wolfe brought this document to him. He did not tell us how he recognised it or anything. He says he signed it and gave it back to Mr. Wolfe. Now let us imagine that to be true; what would Mr. Wolfe do with it? He would take it to the English Consul, the English Consul would write a dispatch to the authorities and send it in; the authorities would refuse to have anything to do with it, and it would be sent back. There would be a dispatch from the English Consul and a dispatch from the Chinese authorities. They have not produced the dispatch from the authorities, nor the dispatch from the Consul, and I have had the records of the Consulate searched and found nothing about it.

Mr. Hayllar—My learned friend has kept out these documents.

Mr Hannen—No, not this. A formal dispatch of this kind sending the deeds in I have expressly admitted. It is not to be found, that is the real truth. Well, that is so far as the $800 deed is concerned. Now, then, we come to the $500 deed. What do they produce as the evidence of what the $500 deed contained? They produce a copy, which is only authenticated by the priest, who says on looking at it—and if your Lordship recollects he did not take very long to look at it—he says, "This is exactly like the one I signed in character; the characters are all alike," and when I asked him how often he had seen it he said once. Now I ask your Lordship whether it is possible to believe that?

Mr. Hayllar—We have produced the dispatch about this.

Mr. Hannen—I have not said you did not produce the dispatch about this.

Mr. Hayllar—But you kept it out.

Mr. Hannen—And I am giving you the reason why I kept it out. With regard to the $800 deed we know nothing. The $500 deed we do know something about. I don't know whether it is a correct copy. I believe it is not a correct copy. With regard to that it is a mere question of memory, but the only person who in any way testifies to the accuracy of that deed is the priest, and the priest says he only saw it once and he says off-hand it is a correct copy, and that I maintain is no proof of its being a correct copy in any way whatever. Well, with regard to the $500 deed, we say we have not got in reality a proper attestation of its truth, and there are certain points about it which I may refer to hereafter which show that in reality the deed is not a correct copy of the deed which we sent in. I am bound to say, however, that with regard to the main difference, the difference in the amount, $500 or $ 500, which my client thinks was the consideration money, but he cannot be certain—when you have to deal with a person of the character of the priest, who came here to acknowledge that he had on one, on two, on three several occasions, endeavoured to defraud the directors of the temple of money—when you have such a gentleman as that to deal with, and Mr. Wolfe not being at that time able to read Chinese characters, it is not impossible there may be some difference introduced, some further fraud on the part of the priest, which we are not able to explain. However, I don't think it is very material. What is certain is that we only have his testimony as to the accuracy of the deed and that my client denies the accuracy of it. Now my learned friend has produced this document, this copy, from a set of records which come from the Chinese authorities. No doubt they come from the proper authorities, who have their custody, but I would point out to your Lordship that they are very different from the ordinary records which are kept of transactions of this kind.. For instance, in the English Consulate, the documents relating to various transactions follow one another in chronological order, whereas the whole of these deeds are collected together with respect to this case. Now, I don't for one moment insinuate against the high Chinese authorities any endeavour to introduce into the case anything that cannot be brought there, but I say that when a case is being prepared for my learned friend there must of necessity be a number of subordinates employed in the work. When this is so we often find the over zeal of such people carrying them away. How often have we heard it remarked in England that when a policeman or detective is set to find out a certain thing he invariably finds it out. So in this case, when a series of documents have to be arranged to complete a case a subordinate officer may find, either from his own imagination or recollection, a copy which is only an emanation from his own brain.

. Mr. Hayllar—That is to say, a forgery.

Mr. Hannen—You may use what hard terms you like about your clients; I try to avoid them. I say such a thing is possible, and that when you don't in the least account for how the original of the $800 deed came into your possession—I say when my learned friend does not account for that and does not account for the copy of the $500 deed, I am entitled to make remarks upon that fact, and the least my learned friend can do is to sit by and hear them. Now, of course, my learned friend will make, as he indeed promises to make, a strong remark on the fact that I have refused to admit the documents, which are copies, I believe, of things which are in the English Consulate. Now, with regard to that it is rather on the principle which I may express as *omne ignotum pro diabolo*. I don't know what they have in them, and I am not going to have introduced into the case, if I can help it, things I don't know anything about, which I have not had time to consider, and which my learned friend knows will make in his favour. After listening to his opening and seeing the kind of argument he makes out of a few words in one deed, I don't wish to give him the opportunity to go into another two hours' dissertation as to what is the meaning of a few words in another document. Under these circumstances I think I am excused if I exclude from the case documents which are not fairly within it, and I think your Lordship will uphold me in the argument that the Chinese, having brought this case into an English court of law, should be bound by the strict rules of evidence. That is all I wish to apply to them, and that is all your Lordship has applied, and as long as that is so I don't think my learned friend can have any complaint. But beyond that, there is a strong practical objection to importing into the case documents of this kind. Things used to be and possibly are—I don't say here now, but at any rate in days gone by things were conducted in a lax, loose manner. Now, it is of importance that this laxity should not be brought to bear to influence one party or the other in litigation. What is the effect of this cross-communication between three or four parties in reference to one transaction? On the one side are the clients of my learned friend and on the other are mine. The authorities put in their own way what they have to communicate to his clients and the Consul puts in his own way what he has to communicate to my client, and very often they come to a misunderstanding, and I say if you bring into the case these documents which are interchanged between the parties you import a further amount of insecurity in all the transactions which took place between them. Here are things said which are never communicated to my client, and which would possibly have been binding upon him if my learned friend had succeeded in introducing them. Under these circumstances, I think it is only reasonable I should exclude from the consideration of the Court these documents which, according to the strict rules of evidence, are not admissible. I don't know in the least what the communications were between the plaintiffs and the Chinese authorities with regard to the 1867 deed, but there is one thing apparent, namely, that they made an important alteration which was in no way communicated to my client. My learned friend lays great stress on the fact that they struck out the words about the option of the lessees. That was never communicated to my client in any way, and therefore it is important to keep out of the consideration of the court things which may possibly lead the court, or a superior court if the case should go to one, to consider that things had been communicated between the parties which never were as a fact communicated to my client. Now, my lord, I pass to the subject of the encroachments. I ask your Lordship to look at the new plan and to say upon it what the whole of the encroachments amount to. There is this pencilling in here which represents, as the plaintiffs allege, the site of the old house. With regard to that they have not proved that one inch of the alleged encroachment is within their grounds; in fact I think it will appear that not one inch is within; it is encroachment outside, and therefore they have no right to complain. But with regard to that, as I have been obliged to go into this as against the whole world, I shall show to your Lordship that that is absolutely and entirely false; that this present house stands upon less ground than the old one. The old one was a bungalow, as everyone in the city knows except that unfortunate priest, who came and told us it was a two storey house. It has now been converted into a two storey house and possibly contains more cubic space. Now, with regard to this other encroachment relating to the wall outside, if your Lordship looks at the pencil line the priest has drawn, you will see it is a matter of a few feet. I shall be able to prove that that is a mistake and that the present wall follows the exact line of the old one. But it is true there is a corner here—of course it is a very serious thing to acknowledge—where we may have encroached five or six inches, and that is the whole of the question of this encroachment so far as it concerns us It is a question as to whether a corner should be round or square. There is a place where the man who built this last wall brought up one and brought down the other and they met at an angle; in the other it was a curve, and the amount of encroachment I believe is about a square foot. That my clients are bound to admit after going carefully through it with their witnesses. They come to this corner and they shake their heads, and they say "Yes, six inches has been encroached upon."

His Lordship—Do you say that was land belonging to the temple?

Mr. Hannen—Yes, so far as we know. If my learned friend comes forward and says it does not, all we can say is—"You let it to us." The evidence I shall offer to your Lordship upon the point—I am now speaking of the mere encroachment, I have not come to the point about the parcels yet—is that of persons who have seen the wall in the old days and people who have seen it now, and of the ordinary run of people a great many can of course, know nothing as to how it came into possession of the defendants. I am now speaking of the evidence I shall bring to show the wall has not been put out as the priest says it has. The evidence I shall use with regard to that I think is conclusive. I shall be able to produce the workmen who did the work, Mr. Wolfe himself, Mr. Stewart, who superintended the pulling down of the one wall and the putting up of the other, and perfectly independent persons who were in the habit of visiting it. Things which were put against the old wall are there still, the roots of old vines, bits of what is called chunam, which were against the old wall in a square, and which are there still in the very same place. With regard to this very portion which my learned friend lays stress on as an encroachment, that was only lately pulled down. That portion was naturally damaged by rain and so on, and the pulling down of a portion of the wall adjoining it, but that was never pulled down until the mason himself came and put up the present wall on the very spot where the old one ran. That was put up squarely on the line where the old one stood, for it was only a few months after the latter had been pulled down.—The learned counsel produced two photographs of the place, one an old one and the other taken a few days ago, as a confirmation of his statement on this point. He also said it had the additional value that it proved that the old house was a bungalow and that there were out-buildings running out towards the north-west. He continued—Now, when I tender my evidence on that point, I have not the remotest doubt what the decision of the court will be as to the including of more ground than before. The present wall does not include a scrap more ground than the old one, or perhaps I ought not to say a scrap more, because there are the six inches.

Mr. Hayllar—We admit there was a wall in 1869.

Mr. Hannen—Within a few inches of the present one?

Mr. Hayllar—Within a short distance—where the priest marked it.

Mr. Hannen—He has marked a good deal more than six inches.

Mr. Hayllar—Well, there it is; of course, my learned friend will try to make it worth as little as he can.

Mr. Hannen—Now, to come to this question of the parcels. With regard to that the state of the case your Lordship will remember was this. Mr. Wolfe came here in the year 1862. Messrs. Welton, Fearnley, and Jackson had all gone. He did not know them personally at all, he did not know from his own knowledge anything they did. When he came here Mr. Smith was the only missionary who lived upon those premises and he was and appeared to be the tenant of a series of buildings and certain land. Now, with regard to that I shall be able to show that the whole of the enclosing wall, as it now stands, was in existence, I believe, then, but certainly before 1867, when the present agreement was made. Mr. Wolfe comes here and he sees Mr. Smith in occupation of certain premises and certain land. He is told, for at that time he had not the management of affairs, that these are held in a certain way; there is a certain agreement made with Fearnley and Jackson and a verbal agreement as to another piece of ground.—The learned counsel read from the deeds the description of the premises let and described on a model in wood which he had had made their several positions. He proceeded—The piece of ground on which the college now stands is the piece we thought was let to Mr. Smith for $12 a year and we used it formerly as a garden.

Mr. Hayllar—Ah, as a garden!

Mr. Hannen—As a fact, although it was used as a garden, if that is the point my learned friend is alluding to, houses were at various times built on it. Before Mr. Smith had it, or before he paid the rent for it, certain small buildings were upon it. After he paid the rent for it he put small buildings on it, and after Mr. Wolfe came into occupation and before the agreement of 1867, Mr. Wolfe put small buildings upon it, such as cow-houses. That was the way that up to that time it had been used. Now, of course, it is impossible for me or my clients to say that all the persons who preceded him in the occupation of that place did not extend the domain which was placed under them, because it is simply surmise whether they did or not, but it is at least reasonable to suppose they did not go and inclose land they had no right to. But Mr. Wolfe comes into possession of a whole lot of buildings and land enclosed together, and he comes to the conclusion these are the premises entire which are covered by these deeds and agreements. It is also to be observed that in the year 1865, according to the petition, "After an inspection of the *locus in quo* on the part of the local authorities the prayer of the said petition was granted." The prayer was as to a wall, and this wall is the consequence of it and it touches the wall which we say had been in existence for some years. Mr. Ting, the Prefect, came and inspected the place carefully three or four times. I think he says he sent a wei-yuen, a sub-ordinate officer, in official costume; they all saw this place and not one word of objection was raised as to this wall, which was in existence at that time.

Mr. Hayllar—He says there was not one.

Mr. Hannen—He says he does not remember it, which is a very different thing, and I think, although it is years ago, he must have had very poor eyesight if he did not see it, but we shall be able to prove conclusively that the wall was in existence. Also the wei-yuen who came and inspected the place must have seen where that wall was, and no complaint was made. The lease of 1866 is then made with great care, all the persons coming and having a most careful survey of the ground, as they say. Well, if they had a careful survey of the ground at the back it seems almost impossible they should not have seen the whole of the enclosure as it then existed, but not one word of complaint is then made. In 1867 they make a lease in which the parcels are described.—The learned counsel pointed out on the model the places which the other side said they let to them, and proceeded—Now, they may possibly have wished to let us a set of things like that, but is it the least likely my client would have taken a lease which was a fresh agreement, a starting afresh, so that things should be quiet and peaceable, of three bits of land perfectly disunited and from which you could not get from one to another?

His Lordship—What did you want the lease for?

Mr. Hannen—He wanted one document to show for land which he was holding under three deeds, and according to their story what they let to him was a very much smaller lot than he was then holding. There is another point which I wish to advert to in passing. Here is their old plan. The point I wish to call your Lordship's attention to is that upon their own showing they have a right to let land outside the walls. The Fang Ko Tien is outside the walls, that small bit the priest marked is outside the walls. If it is a question of right their right has been asserted by themselves and they cannot deny it. They have a right to let land outside the temple. By the agreement of 867 they let that small bit of ground which was rented to Mr. Smith for $12 a year they say. What I say is that my learned friend's argument, saying they could not let this piece because it did not belong to them, falls to the ground, because they did let to us this piece, which is outside the temple grounds. That they did do it is what they absolutely prove by their case.

Mr. Hayllar—But unfortunately the priest had absconded, and we did not know what it was.

Mr. Hannen—They let us something, then, without knowing in the least what they were letting, and because it might possibly be something they did not care about. I don't think that story would hold. I think that when the directors went about the thing with the care they did they must have known what they were doing, and when they let a piece of ground formerly let to Mr. Smith they only had to go to anyone about the place and they would have seen it was this piece on which the college stands. My client believed, and believes now, that piece was Smith's bit, it was let to him by the plaintiffs, it was included in the agreement, and we stand on it. The only other remark upon that part of the case I have to make is that my learned friend did not directly prove by any evidence that they had not a right to let gronud outside contiguous to the temple. He never put the direct question to any of the directors whether they had any right to deal with land outside contiguous to the temple. The only evidence on the point is Ting's evidence, which is that the whole of the grounds and the whole of the temple belong to the Emperor. What he meant by that is very clear; the whole of the land in China does in theory belong to the Emperor, but he did not intend to say that other people had no right to deal with it. We come now to the consideration of the legal effect of this agreement. As I wish as much as possible to shorten what I have to say as to the case, it would be better perhaps to leave that until I have got my evidence before the court. It has not much to do with the evidence; it is purely dry legal argument, and will come better in my summing up. What I contend for is that the lease of 1867 was intended to include everything held by the missionaries at the time of the making of it, that it was intended to give a tenure at least as good as that upon which the land had been held before, and we contend that if it does not do this much, both as to the ground and as to the nature of the tenure, it does not carry out the intentions of the parties. We say that in reality, if the proper construction is put on that lease, it does carry out the intentions of the parties, but if my learned friend's construction is adopted it will not carry out the intention of the parties, and we say if it has been so framed as not to include everything which we held at the time it was made and not to give us as good a tenure as our predecessors had, that has been contrived against us.

Mr. Hayllar—Predecessors?

His Lordship—What do you mean by predecessors?

Mr. Hannen (laughing)—If there is any particular meaning attached to the word "predecessor" which binds me I deny that is what I mean.

His Lordship—Predecessor in title you mean.

Mr. Hannen—But that is not what I was meaning at the moment. My learned friend is so very able in drawing out conclusions from very small facts that I don't want to give him the opportunity. What I mean is that there were people before Mr. Wolfe. Now, my Lord, I say that being the case, even supposing my learned friend were to make out his case is correct, no court of equity would enforce the view he takes. No court of equity would insist upon a construction such as my learned friend puts upon this document, seeing the way in which it was obtained. My lord, when I shall have called my witnesses and once more addressed your Lordship on the subject, I shall have done all that is necessary for me to do in laying the matter before the court. There is not the slightest doubt that, whatever may have been the circumstances that have led to the present case, your Lordship will determine in a fair and equitable manner, and I only hope your decision will be as satisfactory to my learned friend's clients as I have no doubt it will be to mine.

His Lordship, referring to Mr. Hannen's application made on the conclusion of the plaintiff's case that the petition be dismissed, said his ruling was only as to the 4th paragraph of the prayer.

Mr. Hannen having again stated the grounds on which he made his application as to the other paragraphs of the prayer,

His Lordship said he could not rule the point now, it must remain open for the present.

The Rev. John R. Wolfe, the defendant, was then called. He said—I first came to Foochow in 1862, in the month of April. Mr. George Smith, a missionary belonging to the Church of England Missionary Society, was in Foochow at that time. There was no other Missionary belonging to the Society. Shortly after my arrival I went to reside at Wu Shih Shan, at the Tao Shan Kwan. What is now the girls' school was then Mr. Smith's residence. It was in the same state as it is now, with the exception of a kitchen to the north, which has been built since. The Mission house at that time consisted of a long bungalow with a verandah at the west end and two rooms at the north-west corner. Those two rooms extended very nearly out to the door in the wall on to the green patch of grass. In connection with that house Mr. Smith occupied the ground at the back and extending to the site of the college which was burnt down last year and including it. There was a cross wall which ran across part of what is now the kitchen garden running from the Fang Ko Ting northwards to another wall. As to the grass plat the verandah extended over part of it and the North-west corner of it was occupied by the two rooms spoken of. The rest was a small flower garden. At the other side of the wall (the west side) there was a deep hole, apparently made by people digging sand out of it. From that point down about half way was broken and rocky land, and at the lower end was a flat portion of ground on which the ruins of the college now stand. Between the cross wall and the place where the ruins stand there was a small level space about half way. I afterwards built a cow-house on that piece of land. t reached the rock on one side and the wall on the other. The lower piece of ground where the ruins now stand was then a grass plat. I remember an old cow-house and stable that Mr. Smith had erected, that is, they were there when I arrived. All the land I have spoken of was enclosed by a mud wall. At the upper end that wall joined on to the out-houses at the north-west. What is called the Morrison house was also occupied by Mr. Smith. At that time that consisted of four rooms straight in with the kitchen built outside at the front. It was at that time a bungalow. You got from that house out towards the west by steps decending to a door which opened out on the hill. Mr. Smith had purchased a small piece of ground to the north at the bottom of the hill, where the present stable stands. That was enclosed by the remains of an old wall, the roots of old trees, and bamboos. The present wall stands on the site of the old wall as to a part of it. About one third of the grounds within this wall, starting from the east end, had been purchased by Mr. Smith. He never had the deeds with regard to that purchase registered. They were not sent to the Consulate nor was the seal of the Haukwan magistrate put upon them. They had the tepao's stamp put upon them. The first alteration after I arrived was the putting on of the second storey of the Morrison house. I think that was in the spring or summer of 1873. I don't remember whether there were other rooms added below; as far as I can remember there were not. The priest of the temple certainly knew about the alterations being made. I have seen him frequently with the builders and the wood which was used was stored facing the Mo Shan Kwan temple for protection. The alterations took three or four months in making. I never heard of any objection being made to them. The next alteration was the erection of the wall at the north of the Morrison house, which was erected by leave of the authorities in 1865. I applied to Mr. Hewlett, in consequence of the nuisances caused by beggars and other matters for permission to erect this wall to keep out the thieves and beggars and to have a door put up. I don't remember whether the application was in writing or not; I think it was verbal. I obtained the permission applied for. In connection with the matter I saw a seretary from the Board of Trade who came and examined the place. The first looked round the place and then came and asked me if there were any graves within the ground I wanted to enclose. I told them there were no graves, and then they went away and said they would report on the matter. I obtained the permission from Mr. Hewlett, who told me he had spoken to the ma darins. In consequence of that permission I erected a wall and put a door in the wall and erected two gates, one at the north-east and one at the north-west. The gates were erected at the same time as the wall. I frequently saw the wei-yuen afterwards. He came to the house on the next kite-flying day and noticed the wall and gates. At that time the authorities used to send an officer to protect the premises on kite-flying day. The wei-yuen approved of the wall and gates, and said we ought to have had that done long ago as it would have saved him a good deal of trouble. The Consular interpreter saw the wall and the gates. There was a path leading by the side of the house which was stopped up. It was by this way the beggars came in and it was this path we applied for leave to stop. When I was erecting the wall some one came forward and claimed the land. I asked him to produce his title deeds and he produced some old deeds. I purchased the bit of land from him and kept the title deeds. I had them sealed only by the tepao. As we had got authority to enclose the land I did not think it necessary to send the deeds to the magistrate for his stamp. This was in 1865. Between my arrival at Foochow and the year 1867 the ground between where the hole was and the place where the college stands had been altered. I filled up the hole with earth. I cannot say who put up the cross wall above the hole, but I believe it was put up by Mr. Welton. In 1863 or 1864 I took down that wall, and in 1868 I erected the present cross wall. Mr. Mahood arrived in Foochow at that time and occupied Mr. Morrison's house. There was a door in that wall through which the people came from the hill, and I erected the lower cross wall to prevent the people roaming on to the garden and to separate the houses. During the whole of this time the outer wall was never touched. I lived in the old Mission house, which was burnt down in December, 1870. The old house covered a larger area than the present house. Towards the east the old bungalow extended to the wall of the Lee-chow-kung temple; to the west it extended twelve or fifteen feet beyond the west end of the present house; towards the south about five feet beyond the present house. I ha e special means of remembering it did extend further at the south-west corner, because there is a tree standing there between which and the old house there was hardly sufficient space for a man to pass through and now the space is much larger. On the north side, as far as I recollect, the present house extends seven or eight feet beyond the former house. In 1876 I pulled down the wall to the north-west. I did not pull down the southernmost end of it, and it has never been pulled down since I came to Foochow. Later on I had the wall re-erected. It was re-erected on the foundation of the old wall. When it was re-erected you could tell where the old one had stood. There were landmarks. Inside there were vines which I had planted in 1864. One vine is still standing just above the cr ss-wall and there is also a root. Outside at the north-west corner there is a rock called the Pon-tow, which has never been removed. There is a bend in the wall here which causes the passage between the rock and the wall to be a little narrower than before. The wall has been thrown out about half a foot. With this exception the present wall is in the same position as the old one. The whole of the land now enclosed was enclosed when I arrived in Foochow, with the exception of the half-foot of which I have spoken and the piece which was permitted to be enclosed by the authorities in 1865.

The further examination of this witness was adjourned until ten o'clock on the following morning.

(SEVENTH DAY, May 8th.)

The examination in chief of the defendant was continued. He said—I do not remember early in 1866 any proposition as to the purchase of the property then occupied by me. I remember a proposition made as to the purchase of a place known as the Blind Man's Temple. An attempt was made by me to purchase that temple, and the attempt failed. As far as I can now recollect what was done was this—we wanted the Blind Man's Temple to convert it into a yard as the wall of the temple then came up to the existing school. There was a thin lath and plaster partition between the girls' school and the Blind Man's Temple. I asked some one to ask the priest if he could sell the temple. It was at that time in a very dilapidated state. It was used by the blind men once or twice a year. The priest came to my house and said he would sell it, that he had asked the permission of some one—I think he meant the heads of the Blind Man's Association—and that they wanted to build a temple at another place. As far as I recollect the price I offered was $400 for the out and out purchase of it. The negotiation failed. The Taou Shan Kwan people heard of it, I suppose, and they got the priest put in prison. I heard it was the Taou Shan Kwan authorities that pre ented the transaction, but I am not quite sure. I do not remember whether I ever got from the priest any signed deed of sale about this. Between this time and the time of what has been called the $500 deed I made no further attempt to obtain any other purchase. About the time of the attempted purchase of the Blind Man's Temple nor before that time had I made any attempt to purchase the whole of the land occupied by me. I have read through the translation of the $800 deed mentioned in the 10th paragraph of the petition. I never had such a deed drawn up. The evidence of the priest Chun Yuen Ching upon this deed in his examination-in-chief is, so far as I remember, untrue. If what he says had occurred and I had attempted to enter into a deed of this kind I certainly must have recollected it. A little time after the attempted purchase of the Blind Man's Temple there was some transaction as to the purchase of the whole of the premises then occupied by me. As far as I remember, the priest came to my house and we had some conversation about the Blind Man's

Temple, and the failure of the transaction, and he said he was willing to sell me the property which we held under the old lease. I said I was willing to buy if the property could be transferred to me by legal authority. I agreed then, as far as I can now recollect, to purchase the property for $1,500, and as far as I remember I asked my teacher to make a draft of a deed of purchase of the property, to be taken by the priest to be copied in triplicate. The priest took the draft away and brought it back in triplicate, and I sent it in the ordinary course to Her Majesty's Consul. I paid the priest part of the purchase money, $500, when he brought the copy. I think I paid him in two instalments. As far as I remember he said it was inconvenient to take away the $500 at once. The Consul sent the copies back to me for my signature. Mr. Carroll was the Consul. I sent them back to him signed, and the next I saw or heard of them was that they came back to me in two or three months with a note from Mr. Carroll. I have not got the letter received from Mr. Carroll. After receiving back the deeds I sent for the priest and informed him of the fact that the deeds had been returned to me with a note from Mr. Carroll saying the purchase could not be effected. I asked him to hand me back the money I had given him, the $500. He said he had not got it, that he had sent it. I told him that if he could not give me back the money I should inform the Consul. He begged me not to do this, and then promised to give me a promissory note. He brought me a promissory note for $500 either on that day or the next. I cannot say whether the translation of the note in the petition is correct, but I think it is in substance correct. I am perfectly certain I paid him the money the very day he brought me the deeds in triplicate. As to the deed of 1867, I heard from the Consul, Mr. Sinclair, that a new deed was to be drawn up which should include the whole property; that was, as far as I understood it, the whole property within the walls. That was the first intimation I had of it. I have heard that the words "That it should be at the option of the lessee to continue the hiring of the houses" were struck out. I had no intimation that this was to be done. I think it was in consequence of my trouble with the priest in reference to the $500 that this new document came about. I sent the note to the Consul. I am not sure whether the information from the Consul about the new deed came by letter or in conversation. If it came by letter I have not got the letter. I don't remember refusing to pay the rent, in fact I don't remember any one calling for the rent, but I had a letter from the Consul. I have not now got that letter. I said in answer that as the priest had got the $500 and had run away, the rent should be allowed to remain in my hands until the $500 was paid up, and asked him if he did not think that was reasonable. He wrote back to say he did not think it was reasonable, and I at once paid the rent. After that the agreement of 1867 was drawn up. Before the drawing up of this document it was never suggested to me I was to hold any part of the property on a different tenure from that I held it on before.

Mr. Hannen asked the witness if he considered his tenure under the agreement of 1867 was equivalent to the tenure under which he held under the various previous arrangements.

Mr. Hayllar objected to the question on the ground that the document spoke for itself.

The objection was allowed.

Mr. Hannen—Had you known that an alteration in the terms of the agreement of 1850 was to be made would you have signed that deed.

Mr. Hayllar objected to this question also, and the objection was allowed.

Examination continued—I know nothing of any negotiations having taken place with the high authorities in England in 1878, as stated in the 24th paragraph of the petition. If any such negotiations did take place, I had nothing to do with them. If by the high authorities in England is meant the Church Missionary Society, they had nothing to do with it. Mr. Smith died, I think, in September, 1863. He died suddenly at Amoy and his papers were left in disorder.

Cross-examined by Mr. Hayllar—The Church Missionary Society is a voluntary society. It possesses no charter nor anything of that kind, nor does it come under the Charitable Trusts Act. The members, I believe, are the annual subscribers.

In reply to a question as to the constitution of the governing body of the society, the witness produced the rules and regulations.

Cross-examination continued—Messrs. Welton and Jackson were appointed under these rules, I suppose, as I have been. I was not here in 1 70 when the house used as a residence was accidentally burnt down, nor was I here while the present one was being built. It was built by Mr. Mahood. I don't know whether any authority or permission was asked as to its having that top storey.—With your great knowledge of the Chinese, is not that a kind of building that you think would offend their prejudices a good deal? I don't know. I have never heard any objection against it at all. —Do you suspect that it would? It may offend some people.—Is it not offensive to their superstitious, as we will call them? I cannot say.—Have you any suspicions that it is? I have heard some people say that it is, some of the gentry.—You have been told so by the gentry? The gentry have not told me, but the mandarins said the gentry objected to it on the ground of fung shui. I heard this from some of the mandarins who came on to the hill on the occasion of the examination of the ground on the day of the riot, the 30th August last.—If you had been here, Mr. Wolfe, do you think you would have erected a house so elevated as that? I don't think I should.—You were here, I think, when the top storey was put on what is called Morrison's house? Yes, I was.—Did you ask the authorities of the city or your consul for permission to do that, or did you do it entirely without consultation with them? I did not ask.—Why not? I had not the management of the property then at all.—Did anybody ask? I don't know. —Don't you think you should have known? I don't think so. The upper storey was put on in 1863. The house had been turned into a school before I came here, and when I arrived the school had been broken up. The present girls' school was turned into a school in 1876 or 1877. Before that it was a residence. I don't think any permission was asked to turn it into a girls' school. I asked no permission from anybody.—The witness points out the cross-wall he stated in his examination-in-chief he put up to prevent people who came from the hill going through the garden.—I did not ask anybody's permission to put up that wall. The people had not a perfect right to go through the garden into my compound. I considered it private property.—And over whose property did you erect that cross-wall, did you consider? I fancied it was rented from the priest.—Did you make any inquiry? Yes.—From whom? From Mr. Smith, before he died.—How long after Mr. Smith's death did you put up the wall? Mr. Smith died in 1863, and I erected the wall in 1868.—And during these five years the people had been in the habit of going across that property? No.—I thought you said they had? What I said was that when Mr. Mahood moved to that house the servants and people who came to see him roamed into the garden.—But did you not say the public came in too? No; I don't think I did. Of course the people who came to see Mr. Mahood came from the hill; there is no doubt about that. —Now, about the mud wall which you say has always been there; you say you found that in existence when you came? Yes.—That was a low mud wall? No; it was not a low mud wall. It was the same height as now.—Do you know who put it up? I cannot tell who put this part of it up; it was all built before I came in.—I suppose you have not any deed, or any permission from the Prefect, or anything of that kind to show your title to that particular wall? No; I have nothing to show my title to that wall.—Now, going back to the mission house, when that house was built in 1871 was not the situation of the gate which you speak of as having been put up in 1865 when the Prefect gave you permission to erect that other wall removed further east? No.—Was there not a certain riot about it at the time; don't you remember the people coming round about and insisting on the gate being removed and complaining of the right of way being stopped? I never heard of such a thing. You must remember I was in England. —Now you told us about that wall being pulled down, what we called the mud wall, in 1876; had you not at that time bought a piece of property outside, to the north-west, from a Buddhist priest called King Po? I rented it.—Then you threw out your west wall so as to include that piece of land, did you not? Yes.—There was a great deal of difficulty about it? Not at the time.—But there was a complaint to the Consul on the subject, was there not? Not about putting up the wall; I wanted to erect a house on the piece I had rented from the priest and it was then the trouble arose.—Then the matter was referred to the Consul, was it not, in 1876? Yes.—And the result was that you were enjoined to pull down that wall? Yes.—You had to do that on the ground that the piece you had enclosed was public ground? I don't think so.—Were you not informed by the Consul that you had enclosed a piece of public land? I don't think so. I am not sure. —Are you sure you were not? I don't remember that he told me I had enclosed a piece of public ground.—But don't you know that was the ground of the decision? Mr. Pedder, the Acting Consul, told me the mandarins had told him I had attempted to erect a house on a piece of land King Po had no right to let to me.—It led to a great deal of trouble; there has been trouble ever since, has there not? Yes.—Now, with regard to this $800 deed, at the time that that bears date, 1865, you had learnt Chinese, I suppose, pretty well? Very fairly, not very well.

The translation of the deed referred to is as follows:—

A deed of an absolute receipt of rent for a perpetual term made by Chun Yuen Ching, student of a Taouist priest called Lin Yung Mow, at the Taou Shan Kwan Temple on the Wu Shih Shan. Whereas in the 30th year of Tao Kwang (1850) two houses situate on the left hand side of the Taou Shan Kwan temple, one in front and the other at the back, were let to British Missionary Welton for building a house for residence, at an annual rent of $100, and subsequently a piece of ground was also let to him at an annual rent of $32. Now British Missionary Mr. Wolfe being desirous of making an absolute payment of rent for a perpetual term, doth hereby pay $300 as a payment in full of the rent for the term above mentioned. Therefore neither Chun Yuen Ching nor any of the other priests at the temple shall from henceforth collect any more rent. If Mr. Wolfe should return to England, neither Chun Yuen Ching himself, nor any of the other priests at the temple, shall call to collect rent from any of the missionaries, whoever they may be. The boundary of the ground of the premises given in the following is agreed to by Chun Yuen Ching, that is, in front thereof it abuts on the edge of the main road in front of the Taou Shan Kwan; at the back thereof on the main road leading to Wan Chang Kung temple; on the left hand side thereof (east) on the edge of the road by the wall of the Ne Toh Sze Monastery; and on the right hand side thereof (West) on the wall of the Pau Leong Tang Monastery. The boundary on the four sides being distinctly specified, and the sum of $300, being the whole amount of rent for a perpetual term, having been this day received in full by Chun Yuen Ching, he (Chun Yuen Ching) nor any of the other priests at the Taou Shan Kwan Temple shall from henceforth give no cause of troubles, or call to collect any more rent. Fearing words of mouth will not afford evidence, this deed of an absolute receipt of rent for a perpetual term is therefore drawn to serve as proof, and a copy of an agreement of rent is also given up as proof.

(Signed) CHING WOO KUN, witness Tepao's stamp.

(Signed) CHUN YUEN CHING maker of the above deed of an absolute receipt of rent for a perpetual term.

Tung Chi, 4th year, 12th moon, 17th day.

Could you have read that deed do you think? I cannot say; I would have had the help of my Chinese teacher.—Could you have read it without the help of your teacher? No.—Could you not have read that in 1865? Not by myself, but with the help of a teacher.—Were you in the habit of going through your documents with your teacher? Not always.—But were you in the habit of reading them? Yes.—Then you must have seen that in the agreement of rent of 1867 the words about the option of the lessees were omitted. You must ha e improved in your studies between 1865 and 1867. Perhaps you had advanced so for as to be able to do without the help of a teacher? No.—But you could have read the agreement of rent of 1867 with the aid of a teacher? Yes.—Did you do so? I think I read it through.—Could you write Chinese then? No; not well.—Then when you wanted any drafting done, or any documents drawn, I suppose you got your teacher to do it? Yes, I think that would be the ordinary way.—Well, when that $400 transaction about the Blind Man's Temple was on the *tapis*, was there any document drawn up about it; were the terms reduced as a preliminary to writing? I don't remember.—But really, this comes to be of great importance. I must ask you to charge your memory if you can as to whether that transaction about the Blind Man's Temple was reduced to writing by anybody? I cannot say; it may have been done or it may not.—If it had been done for you it would ha e been done by your teacher, would it not? Most probably.—He would have shown it to you? Probably he would.—And perhaps not? Perhaps not.

By his Lordship—My teacher's name was Ting. He was a literary man. I really don't know what has become of him. I think he is in the city somewhere.

Cross-examination continued—Are you quite sure he did not write that? I really cannot say.—Had your teacher anything to do with your interviews with the p iest, Chun Yuen Ching, about this Blind Man's Temple; was he present? I think he knew of the general idea. I don't think he was present.—I suppose you discussed the matter with your teacher a good deal and that he knew all about what you were wanting? I am not aware I discussed it with him; he knew I wanted to buy the place.—Did you discuss it with him? No, not particularly.—But at all? I told him I wanted to buy it.—And your negotiations with the priest took place personally? Yes.—And you cannot say whether the $400 agreement was reduced to writing by your teacher or any one else? I really cannot say now.—Can you swear, looking at that $800 document, that you never saw it before? I dare not swear I saw it before.—My question was that you never saw it before? I don't think I ever saw it before.—But I want something more than that. I want to know whether, with your power of reading Chinese, you can swear you never saw that document? I swear that I have not the slightest recollection of ever seeing this document.—Or any document about the Blind Man's Temple? I don't remember seeing any such document.—Well, now, I want to call your attention to this $800 deed. According to the translation we have, which stands uncontradicted, it purports to be a very sweeping document and to convey to you a much larger piece of ground than is conveyed in the $500 deed. What I want to know from you, Mr. Wolfe, is whether you had been at that time negotiating with the priest for the purchase, not only of the property you now hold, but of that included within the boundaries there mentioned? Certainly not; I don't remember.—You don't remember, but will you swear, at this length of time, that the priest is absolutely false when he says you had? I am prepared to go that length.—That the priest was absolutely false when he says you were negotiating for the land with all these boundaries? I have no recollection of it.

His Lordship—That is not Mr. Hayllar's question; you must know that as an educated man.

Witness—Will you put your question again?—The document I produced is the one before you. It is a record of the Government of China. A man comes here and swears that is his signature. The document purports to convey to you the property included within the walls and a great deal outside, and what I want to know is whether you are prepared to swear that man is telling a falsehood when he says you were negotiating with him for the purchase of all that property? I swear he is telling a falsehood.—Just read the name of the signatory there, the witness, Chang Woo Kit; can you read that? I see that.—Now, was he not one of your servants? I don't remember it.—Was he not a water carrier established about your premises? I don't remember it.—Woo Kit, perhaps you called him? I never remember having a man of that name.—You never recollect having such a man in your service as a water carrier? No.—Will you swear you never had such a man? Well, that is hard to swear. I don't remember the man's name. I don't know who he is.—He purports to be the witness to that document, which is an important one? Yes.—He was also called Kow Fo; do you remember having a man of that name in your employment? I don't remember such a man.—Have you got the deeds you received from the man (King Po) when you built that wall without the permission of the Prefect?

Mr. Hannen objected that no notice had been given to produce the deeds.

Mr. Hayllar said Mr. Hannen had stated the previous day that the deeds were in court, stamped by the tepao.

The deeds were produced.

Cross-examination continued—Now, that is the tepao's seal on the deed you got from that man in 1865, which I have not seen until this moment? Yes.—Now, will you just compare these two seals together (the $800 deed and King Po's deed) and see whether they are the same? As far as I can see they are the same, but I cannot be sure.—You cannot be sure! We will see whether that is so. Now, do you know the name of the tepao who signs that? No.—Is it not a universal practice that in any dealing whatever with land the document should first be sealed by the tepao? I believe it is.—He is the headman of the hundred, or district, whose duty it is to look after that business? Yes.—Is not the tepao a man appointed *pro tem* by the District Magistrate; he is the headman of the neighbourhood who gets his appointment from the magistrate, is he not? I think so.

Mr. Hannen—Do you know anything about this arrangement, really?

Witness—No.

Cross-examination continued—Do you not know the tepao's seals are constantly changing, that they are changed with every magistrate that comes in? I don't know.—Don't you know these things are done to guard the revenue of China, when it is necessary the Emperor should know all documents are genuine? I don't know the revenue arrangements of China; I know the tepao exists.—But don't you know the reason these things are sealed is that the Emperor may know where to get his taxes? I don't know.—Have you paid any taxes to the Emperor of China on these documents (the deeds of the land sold by King Po)? No, I have not.—Now, let us come down to what I call the $500 deed. That is a copy I show you. Are you prepared to swear that that is not an absolutely correct copy of the $500 document you made with the priest in every particular? I really cannot swear.—You cannot swear, but is it not? How can I possibly swear at this length of time; I have not the original before me.—Do you impugn that, either yourself or through your counsel; I want to know whether you can swear that is not an absolutely correct copy? I cannot say at all.—Now, in that document occurs these words, "But he, feeling very much the inconvenience of the Taouist priest's calls, is willing to pay to the said priest the sum of $500 in order that he shall never again call to collect the rent." Do you see those words there; can you follow in Chinese? No I don't think I can.—Well, we will point them out to you? Yes, I see here that this deed says I willingly give out 500 Mexican dollars to the priest so that he may not come again for the rent.—The words you see there are "willing to give;" are you sure upon reading those words you did give him $500? I am sure I gave him $500.—That being one transaction, the giving of that deed and the payment of the $500?—Yes; I gave him the $500, I think, in two instalments.—Had you paid $500 in reference to the Blind Man's Temple before? No, I had not.—And yet you knew that transaction had fallen through because it could not be registered? No.—You knew the transaction had fallen through? Yes.—Now, do you mean to say you did not think from that there was a great risk of this falling through? No, I did not.—No risk at all? No, I did not.—You told us just now the directors objected? I heard so.—Then do you mean to say you paid $500 to this priest when you had the risk before your mind? There was no risk in my mind.—Do you mean to say that? You must remember I had rented that property, as I thought, by a lease under which I could never be turned out as long as I paid rent.—Now, do just think, Mr. Wolfe, if you can bring your memory back to the time, if you did not think there was a good deal of risk of that transaction falling through? I did not think there was any risk at all.—Now, you know this man was taken to the yamên to be punished for one of the transactions; you have said it was for the $400 one? Yes.—Don't you know that if a man is punished for a transaction it must be a very bad one in their eyes? I suppose so.—Now, are you sure it was not after the $500 transaction he was taken to the yamên; I shall call your attention to some documents presently? I am quite certain.—Did you go and see Mr. Carroll about it? I spoke to Mr. Carroll about the priest's being imprisoned.—And did not you yourself get Mr. Carroll to intercede? I believe I did.—Now will you swear—because we are on ground we must be very careful about, and it is an important question—will you swear it was not about the $500 transaction you interceded? I swear it was not.—Do you know that letter (letter from Consul Carroll to the Chinese authorities)? No.—Do you know that signature? No, I don't remember it.—Have you any reason to doubt the genuineness of that signature? I don't know anything about it.—Have you never seen Mr. Carroll's signature? I have seen his signature, but I cannot swear whether this is his signature. —I don't ask you to swear; I ask you to say whether you have any reason to doubt it? I don't know anything about it; that is the simple answer.

His Lordship—Is it signed by Mr. Carroll in Chinese?

Mr. Hayllar—In English, my Lord. There is no date to the letter, but the date of receipt is put in.

Cross-examination continued—Now, this is that letter—

(TRANSLATION.)

SIR,—I trust you have duly received the letter I sent you yesterday, and was surprised to find that the Taouist priest Chun Yuen Ching has not been released, whose re'ease is of importance. I personally called upon the Hankwan District Magistrate to-day inquiring of the cause of his (the priest's) still not being released, and received a reply that he dare not himself take the responsibility of discharging him as he has not obtained an order from the Prefect to that effect. After careful consideration of this matter, I see there is no reason why the premises occupied by Mr. Wolfe should not be still rented at a yearly tenancy, though their being rented for a perpetual term is inconsistent with reason. Why should an innocent man be suffering in this matter? It is therefore most sincerely hoped that the Taouist priest Chun Yuen Ching, as well as his student priest, may immediately be released without any further delay. With best wishes.

(Signed) CHARLES CARROLL.

The card of Consul Carrol'.

To the Prefect of Foochow-foo.

I want to know whether, after hearing that letter, you say the priest was not put in prison with reference to letting the premises occupied by you for a perpetual term? It was not after the perpetual lease the priest was punished.—Well, here are the words, it is impossible to misunderstand them: "I see no reason why the premises occupied by Mr. Wolfe should not be still rented at a yearly tenancy, though their being rented for a perpetual term is inconsistent with reason," showing it had nothing to do with the Blind Man's Temple, but the premises rented by you. I want to know whether, after hearing that letter, you adhere to your statement that the priest was imprisoned for the $400 document? I adhere to that statement.

His Lordship—What is the date of that letter.

Mr. Hannen—There is no date.

Mr. Hayllar—I am not putting it in in reference to the date, but to this particular passage.

His Lordship—Is it in evidence?

Mr. Hayllar—No; I am asking in cross-examination.

Cross-examination continued—Now, did you not ask Mr. Carroll to intercede for this priest, Chun Yuen Ching? I did.—When, in what year? I think it was in 1866.—Can you bring to your recollection the date? It was after the transaction about the Blind Man's Temple, and I think it was in March or April, I cannot say positively.—But, Mr. Wolfe, that is a Government record filed by us; it is a matter we know nothing of except from that record; now, do you think Mr. Carroll is playing the fool with the Chinese authorities to send them such a letter? I don't know.—Can you give any reason for the thing, any explanation at all as to why Mr. Carroll should have written that letter? No.—Just consider a moment. Why should Mr. Carroll write to us and say that after careful consideration you may still go on holding these premises? Was not the priest imprisoned because he let you the premises for $500?

His Lordship—Read the document.

Witness—I read it yesterday.

His Lordship—Well, read it again.

Witness reads the document.

Cross-examination continued—After reading that you still say you know nothing about it? I still say I know nothing about it. I know the priest was imprisoned, and I know Mr. Carroll interfered.—Was he imprisoned twice? No, only once.—He was imprisoned for the first offence and not for the second; is that what you say? Yes.

His Lordship—Does he state that as a fact?

Mr. Hayllar—Do you state that as a fact? that he was imprisoned for the $400 transaction a d not for the second one?

Witness—I state that he was imprisoned on account of the transaction about the Blind Man's Temple and not the $500 deed.

Mr. Hayllar—And that you state as a fact of your own knowledge?

Witness—That I state as a fact of my own knowledge.

His Lordship—But look here, Mr. Wolfe, were you in treaty at the time of the $400 transaction for the purcha e of the whole of the premises?

Witness—No, my lord.

His Lordship—What interval was there between the $400 transaction and the purchase you speak of of the whole of the premises in respect of which the $500 was paid on account.

Witness—As far as I can recollect, three or four months.

His Lordship—How long was he in prison with regard to the $400?

Witness—I think, my Lord, no longer than a week.

His Lordship—When did the negotiations for the purchase of the whole of the property commence?

Witness—I really cannot state the exact month. I think it must have been in July or August.

His Lordship—Well, now, Mr. Wolfe, after these answers to me, can you adhere to your statement? Look at that letter again.

Witness—I am certain, my Lord.

His Lordship—Now, be good enough to consider, Mr. Wolfe. We know your sacred position, and we give you credit for recollecting you are under an oath.

Witness—Certainly. I adhere to my statement.

His Lordship—You know you have sworn positively. I will read you my notes of your answers if you like.

Witness—Do you wish me to answer?

His Lordship—Well, I simply want to know if you adhere to your statement?

Witness—Yes, I do.

His Lordship—Then the Consul must have had a sort of prevision as to what was going to take place.

Mr. Hannen—He says he adheres to it.

His Lordship—You see yourself what it is.

Mr. Hannen—He says himself he cannot understand that letter, and there is an end of it.

His Lordship—It appears from what he says that the man must have been liberated long before that letter was written.

Mr. Hannen—Perhaps Mr. Carroll wrote it under a misapprehension.

Mr. Hayllar—Oh, let me read the words—The learned counsel again read the letter.

Cross-examination continued—I suppose you went yourself and told him the priest was not liberated? It is probable I did.—But didn't you? Well, it is quite probable I did.—And that was in reference to the $400 deed? Yes.—Then how could Mr. Carroll know anything about the perpetual lease? I cannot explain it.

His Lordship—Where does that come from?

Mr. Hayllar—From our records. It bears Mr. Carroll's signature and his card accompanies it.

Mr. Consul Sinclair explains to his Lordship that the document in question is a note, and that it is not usual to date notes in China; official communications are dated, but unofficial letters are not dated.

At this stage the court adjourned for luncheon.

On the court resuming, Mr. Hayllar continued his cross-examination. He said—Now, Mr. Wolfe, you have, I suppose, had permission by yourself or your counsel to examine the official records in reference to this case in the Consulate.

Mr. Hannen—I have had premission.

Mr. Hayllar—Well, have you found any reference to this $400 lease or the imprisonment of the priest? I only ask for information.

Mr. Hannen—I am the only person who has looked at the papers and I have made no notes of what I saw. I have asked Mr. Playfair to search carefully for any communication from the Consul to the authorities forwarding the $800 deed and he has informed me, and I purpose proving it, that no such communication is there.

Mr. Hayllar—Most clearly, because it never was forwarded. But I want to know whether there is any reference to this $400 deed or the priest being imprisoned in connection with it.

Mr. Hannen—I have not looked for it, because according to our story it never came to anything at all. Mr. Wolfe's account is that it never went further than preliminaries and therefore it would not appear there according to our view.

His Lordship—Yes, but you have not looked for it?

Mr. Hannen—I have not looked for it.

His Lordship—Then Mr. Hayllar's question was, have you by yourself or counsel examined the records of the Consulate in reference to this matter, that was with regard to the $400 transaction.

Mr. Hayllar—Yes, with regard to the whole transaction—the run of the papers in fact.

Mr. Hannen—There are fifteen volumes of various things, and I am allowed look at anything I like. They are not collected together like my learned friend's.

Mr. Hayllar—But excuse me, we have had to look over a hundred volumes to get these; they are only stuck in for the purposes of this case.

His Lordship—But Mr. Hayllar's question was, have you had permission by yourself or counsel to examine the records of the consulate. Then what does the witness say, does he say yes? But Mr. Hannen says yes.

Witness—I think so, my Lord.

Cross-examination continued—But going through the Taou Shan Kwan property, you knew about the date when this took place? Yes I knew the date.—Well didn't you tell your counsel, or give him some clue to find documents about it? I don't remember.—But this is a very serious question. Did you not give him a clue to look for the documents about the $400 deed if there is such a thing? Yes, I told him the date.

—Did you find anything about the release of the priest, anything whatever? No.

His Lordship—Does he know anything about it, has he ever been near?

Mr. Hannen—No, he has not.

Mr. Hayllar—Well. that is his own fault, if he does not like to look after his own business.

Cross-examination continued—Now, according to you, Mr. Wolfe, that transaction about the $500 deed having fallen through, left the priest in your debt $500? Yes.—That is the way in which you put it; and then in order to repay yourself the $500, as you put it, you made him make this promissory note? I did not make him make it; I asked him to and he promised to.—Well, you asked him to, quite so. Now, you paid $132 a year; that was your rent, was it not? Yes, I think so.—Are you not quite certain? Don't fence with the question. Was not that the rent? Yes.—Well, then, it was the rent. Don't think anything about such questions as that.

His Lordship—You are a witness, Mr. Wolfe; if you know a fact don't say "I think" or "to the best of my recollection." You want to make me believe you are the witness of truth.

Witness—Yes.

His Lordship—Then speak as you suppose a truth-speaker would.

Mr. Hayllar—Then what I want to ask is why you didn't set this rent off against the principal if your object was simply to get back the money? Why didn't you set it off for four years and let it end so, instead of charging $11 per month and making it at the rate of 24⅕ per cent. interest?

His Lordship—I made the calculation here somewhere. It was 26⅖ I think.

Mr. Hayllar—My question is this—If your object was to get back the $500, if your true, honest, real object was to get back that $500, why didn't you merely set off the rent against it and let it be wiped out, instead of letting it be in such a way as in this case—it wipes out the rent for ever.

Witness—When I asked the priest for the $500 he said he had not the money; he had spent it. I told him I should report him to the Consul, and he begged me not to report to the Consul and said that if I did not report to the Consul he would allow the rent to remain as interest on the $500 until such time as he would refund to me the $500. That is the only explanation I can give.

Cross-examination continued—Well, but, Mr. Wolfe, let me ask you this question. This is an old Taouist priest, and he told you he had spent the money. Did you honestly, in your own mind, think that money ever was going to be repaid? I certainly expected, I hoped, he would repay it.—That is not my question. In your heart of hearts, sir, did you think that money ever was going to be repaid? I really cannot say whether the priest intended to repay me or not; I hoped it would be paid sometime.—That is not my question. In your conscience did you think that money was ever going to be repaid or did you think by this promissory note you had got a perpetual hold on that property? I fully thought the money would be paid to me sometime or other by the priest.—With that rate of interest on it? That is all I say.—With that rate of interest? I fully expected the priest would repay me the money; I fully expected he had not spent the money and that he had said he had spent it to avoid payment.—And so to facilitate his repaying it you put that rate of interest on it? He himself put that rate of interest on it and I consented.—You consented, yes? Well, that is the truth, I cannot say anything more.—Let me call your attention to one clause in this document. This document was made in 1866. Your intention was not to go home to England very soon? No, not very soon; two or three years.—Oh, but permanently I mean? No, it was not my intention.—Now let me call your attention to this in the document "None of the missionaries, whoever they be, shall after the return of Mr. Wolfe to England be called upon to pay rent." Now, I ask you if that did not mean in your honest heart an intention on your part to get that property in perpetuity? It certainly was not my intention to get the property in perpetuity by that.—That is your answer? That is my answer.—Well, why did you make the interest such a curious interest, such as two and two per month so as to make it exactly cover the rent? He told me the rent was to be placed over against the $500 until such time as the $500 was refunded; I cannot make it anything more than that.—But you see it is such a curious sum, two and two per month, so as to bring it to exactly that amount. I suppose you had some talk about that amount? Yes.—And how came it to be fixed at this extraordinary rate? The priest himself fixed it.—Oh, but you talked about it with him? Yes, of course I did.—Were you not aware of the fact that if the priest did not pay the money you had the property in perpetuity? No, I was not.—You were not; singular! Now did you send that document to the Consulate to be registered? Certainly not.—It was not a kind of document that ought to be registered, was it? I don't know.—I suppose if it had been you would have sent it, like an honest man? I really don't know, it never struck me.

Mr. Hannen—I really don't know whether we have reached a stage of the case when a question can be put in that form—"as an honest man."

Mr. Hayllar—Yes, but it is a question of accusing us of forgery. You have impugned a document in our records.

Mr. Hannen—We simply say we know nothing about it.

Mr. Hayllar—Because, as you said to me yesterday, you have too much tact to use the word. It has now become a question between us, which is true and which is false, and my duty now is to carry the matter out in a manner I can understand.

Mr. Hannen—There is no reason why you should use words to fluster a witness.

Mr. Hayllar—No; I don't want to.

Mr. Hannen—Then don't do it.

Mr. Hayllar—Then I will put it without.

Cross-examination continued—I ask you now, do you know whether it ought to be registered or not? I don't know.—Did you inquire? I don't know.—Did you think it was your business to inquire when you had a document of this kind? I never thought about it.—It is a matter of such slight importance that you did not inquire? I never thought about it.—'r was it that you did not want to inquire? I never thought about it one way or the other.—Come, let us have a little common sense. Here is a document, the effect of which is that if the priest did not pay this money you had the property free of rent for good and all. Now, I want to know from you whether it never occurred to you that it ought to be brought to the notice of the authorities? It never occurred to my mind; that is the truth.—You were going pretty constantly to the Consulate, if I mistake not? Yes.—Pretty nearly every day, with one complaint or another? I don't say that.—You had a good deal of business in official and missionary matters? I had some business; I won't say it was a good deal.—You have been there very frequently? Yes, I have been there very often.—Did it ever occur to you just to inquire in a friendly way, "I have got this document, it is a matter of some importance, ought it to be registered or not?" Did it ever occur to you? Never.—Then the priest bolted, didn't he? Yes.—There was not much chance of his paying back the money then, was there? None.—Then did you go openly to the persons who were next interested in the matter and say, "I have had this transaction with your old priest; I am not going to pay any more rent?" No, I don't remember having done that.—Did you do it? I will explain to you.—I just want that explained. Did you go openly to the authorities of the city or any one and say, "I have got this transaction, and I am not going to pay any more rent?" No.—You did not; why not? I really cannot say. I waited, I suppose, until I heard from them, from the Taou Shan Kwan people.—Waited till you heard from them, Mr. Wolfe! Didn't you bring to their notice that their priest had gone, having fled from punishment or something else, and that you held a document of this man's? No; not formally.—But in any way whatever? I was going to tell you. One day, standing in the garden, I saw two men connected with the temple, and we had some conversation about the priest, and this note was mentioned. I told them the priest had given me this note for the $500 which I had paid him when he signed the deed. I told them the whole story then. The next thing I heard was when I had a letter from the Consul.—Yes, and the Consul told you to pay the rent? Yes; but I think I had sent the document in the meantime to Mr. Sinclair, complaining of the priest.—You think you had? Yes, as far as I remember.—But what I want to know is this; with this document in your hand, for $500, you got the property in perpetuity. What had you got to complain of the priest about, if he had given you such a bargain as that? Because he went away with the $500.—But you had got this in return, the advantage of never paying any more rent for these premises; what had you to complain about? That he ran away with the money.—But I say you had this splendid equivalent, what had you to complain against him for? Because he ran away with this money.—But you don't answer my question. There is no complaint if he gave you this equivalent. If he ran away once and for all it is clear if that document was to hold good you would never pay any more rent? When he went away of course the rent was to be paid to other people.—Why was it to be paid to other people? As the priest ran away the other priests would have to get the rent.—But, look here, "The rent will not be paid till the loan is refunded, and before the repayment of the said loan neither the Taouist priest himself nor any of the other priests at the temple shall call to collect the rent." Now, what do you say to that; if that was a true document what did it matter whether the priest had run away or not? Of course I can't say.—But what had you to complain of? My question is, if you had got this splendid equivalent for your $500, what had you to complain of? Because I expected when the priest had run away the whole thing had come to an end. I expected when that note was made the priest would have remained in the temple, and I should have received the rent until such time as he paid back the $500. When he ran away then I felt there was no more security for my getting the money, either the rent or the $500. That is all the explanation I can give.—But I am just going to ask you a question upon that. Did not the matter come to the knowledge of the Consul, because the people connected with the temple complained that you did not pay the rent? Did not that bring the whole thing out? Now, just be a little cautious, because I will call your attention to some documents before you answer that question. My question, founded on these documents, is whether it was not a fact that you did not pay the rent, and that put the fat in the fire and brought the thing out once and for all? I will just call your attention to that despatch from Mr. Sinclair to the Taotai. That is the translation, which you can probably read with more facility than you can the Chinese. We have the original here.

Witness—Is it necessary for me to read all through this?

Mr. Hayllar—That is a matter for your own consideration.

Witness—I don't know anything about this. This document was written by the Consul and I don't call it in question at all.

Mr. Hayllar—That is what we call fencing.

Mr. Hannen—He says he does not dispute it. That is not fencing.

Cross-examination continued—I give you this for your own protection, and I ask you whether it was not brought out by your not paying rent? I don't remember any person coming to my house for the rent.

Mr. Hayllar—Then that is neglecting. I put it to you, neglect or refusal?

His Lordship—Did he pay the rent? It is quite possible he may have paid it without anybody calling for it.

Mr. Hayllar—Yes, my question is whether you did not neglect or refuse to pay the rent for the summer quarter after the priest had absconded.

Witness—I did not refuse to pay the rent.

Mr. Hayllar—You see, your neglect may be the same thing.

His Lordship—Was it your non-payment of rent that brought the matter to the notice of the authorities?

Cross-examination continued—Yes; but you did know, as I understand, if your former answers are correct. If you sent a note to Mr. Sinclair you did know. Was it not the fact that you did either neglect or refuse to pay the rent? I don't remember. The only thing I remember about the matter is my having spoken to two of the men of the Taou Shan Kwan Temple. They were on the temple grounds below, and I was in the garden. I spoke to them from the hill, and we had a conversation about the priest and this $500. I think I said to them on that occasion that the rent ought to be left with me until the $500 was paid up. It was not a refusal on my part.—That is just what I come to. You knew the priest had then run away? Of course I did.—Then how were you to be recouped the $500? Did you never hear the Chinese had complained to Mr. Sinclair of your not having paid the summer quarter's rent; did you never hear that, as a fact? I never heard that as a fact, that is, before Mr. Sinclair's letter came to me.—You did know then from Mr. Sinclair that a complaint had been made by the Chinese to that effect? As far as I remember Mr. Sinclair wrote to me to that effect.—And then he having written to you to that effect you paid the rent? I wrote back to Mr. Sinclair.—Oh, but did you pay it? Not then.—Now what I want to know is this, did you never hear the people connected with the Taou Shan Kwan, the directors and others, were very much incensed in consequence of your dealings with the priest? I heard they did not like it when the priest ran away, when they found it out.—When they found it out! Well, when they found it out, as you say, they didn't like it; but didn't you have a talk with with the priest yourself? Didn't he communicate to you the fact that they were very angry with him? I really don't remember; I cannot say whether he did or not.—Did you never speak to him on the subject? You see this is not a light matter; it is a serious matter, and didn't you speak to him upon the question whether the people of the temple did like it or didn't like it? Cannot you charge your memory to that extent? I spoke to him on the matter.—What did you say? I told him he was to refund the $500 to me; if not I would inform the Consul about it.—But later than that, did not the priest came to you and tell you the thing had leaked out and the directors were very angry with him? No; I don't remember his having told me that.—Knowing what you did about his being punished before, didn't you think it was a kind of thing that would make them very angry with him? I really cannot say.—I don't ask you whether you remember; I ask you whether you don't think this was a kind of thing that would make them very angry? Certainly it would, if he had done it without the consent of anybody.

Mr. Hannen—You keep on saying "the thing;" which do you refer to?

Mr. Hayllar—The note; that is a thing.

Witness—I did not understand you to mean the note. I thought you meant the lease.

Cross-examination continued—I mean the whole transaction. Didn't you think that was a kind of business which would make them very angry? If the priest had not authority to sell the property of course it would be a natural feeling in their mind.—No; but to give up the rent in this way, was not that a kind of thing that would make them very angry? I suppose it would. I beg your pardon, I thought you meant the lease.—No, I mean the note; don't you think that was a kind of thing that would make them very angry? I don't think that.—My question is, didn't you think the whole transaction in connection with the $500 note was a kind of business to make the directors very angry when it came to their knowledge? I did not think so at the time.—At the time! Well, then, why didn't you tell them openly?

Mr. Hannen—He has just told us he did tell them openly.

Cross-examination continued—I will ask you this question: didn't you think when that business came out about the promissory note the priest would be liable to punishment, and very severe punishment, if he were found, knowing how he had been punished before? I didn't think so.—Did you take the trouble to inquire into such a matter as that? No.—Now, I want to know again from you, Mr. Wolfe, after that poor old ruined priest, ruined and broken by this transaction, a poor old Taouist priest, it doesn't much matter perhaps, but I want to know whether he didn't come to you in terrible trouble about it and ask your advice? He certainly did not.—Did you not have any inkling that this poor old fellow was going to run away in consequence? I had not the slightest idea.—Did you ever inquire about him? I sent for him as soon as the deeds were sent back from the Prefect.—Very, well. Now then, Mr. Wolfe, I am just coming to another part of the subject for a minute or two. We have come down to 1876, and we have heard that from 1876 you have had a good deal of trouble with the Chinese about buildings and one thing and another. You have, have you not? Yes.—Since 1876 you have had a good deal of trouble with the Chinese? I said some trouble.—About the Taou Shan Kwan property? No.—About other property? About the house I intended to build outside the wall, on the King Po ground.—Then you or some of your colleagues, I dont know which of them, put up that building which was burnt down in 1878? Yes.—Now, in your answer you state with reference to that matter, which is of some considerable importance, "I admit that the college was, with the sanction of Her Britannic Majesty's Consul at Foochow, and without visible objection on the part of the plaintiffs or any other person, erected during the year 1878 on a piece of land enclosed within the said wall." Now. I want to know whether you did get permission from the Consul to erect a building of this kind, such as you put up? Yes.—Have you got the permission you received—I am very anxious to see it? Yes.

Mr. Hannen said he would get the document.

Cross-examination continued—Well, there was so much trouble going on about this building outside the walls that a good many negotiations went on through the Consul about your changing the property in 1877 and 1878? Yes.—There was some negotiation about your going elsewhere, was there not? There was some talk about removing the house outside and giving us another site.—Where was it to go to?

His Lordship—What house?

Witness—Not the house that was burnt down, a house we intended to build in 1876 or 1877.

His Lordship—That is the first we have heard of that.

Mr. Hayllar—Yes; I understood it was about this house that was built.

Mr. Hannen—At first Mr. Wolfe intended to build a house on a piece of land he bought from King Po, and that was squashed, and he built the house he intended to build there on this piece of ground, and in the meantime some negotiation was going on.

Cross-examination continued—Was it not while these negotiations were going on that you continued to go on building this place? No, I am not aware of any negotiations taking place when we built on the piece of land where the ruined house stands.—At the time the lease of 1866 was made, referring to the property outside, were the buildings you have got there now already in progress? Not the buildings. Not part of them. No part of the buildings.—Was there anything in progress? The walls were up.—Well, they are large retaining walls are they not? Mud walls.—Well, you had already got that property under some other documents? Yes.—And these are the documents which are referred to in the lease of September, 1866, as the false deeds, seven in number, given by Hwang Shang Sheng and others? Yes.—Under these deeds, seven in number, you had entered into possession of the property and had put up certain walls; that is what I want to know? Yes, having got this property and the lease from this man we put up certain walls.—Then you sent it to be registered, I suppose. Is this the deed you sent—

A lease of perpetual tenancy entered into by Hwang Shang Sheng who by absolute purchase is in possession of a house and a garden situated at Taou Shan Poo in the Haukwan district. The house is facing the North consisting of two rooms with three window shutters east, a hall, an outhouse, and a sitting room—five rooms in all. It abuts at the front on the main road and at the back on the edge of the road in front of Li Chou Kang Temple, on the left on the house of the Shen family, and on the right on a garden. The roof and rafters above and the ground inclosed in the house walls below are also included. The garden abuts in front on the main road and at the back on the edge of the road in front of the Li Choe Kung Temple, on the left on his own house, and on the right on the house of the Chong family. It measures eight changs and two covids long and nine changs and eight covids broad.

The above house and garden he of his own accord agrees to let to Mr. Wolfe for a perpetual term, the price of which perpetual tenancy, namely, $145, has been paid in full to and received by him this day. The tenants shall be at liberty to pull down anything in the premises and make alterations therto and may, to suit their convenience, build thereupon for dwelling purposes. All the material of the old house such as beams, rafters, door, and window shutters, flooring tiles and bricks, when taken down, shall be taken back by Hwang Shang Sheng. The tenant, after having paid in full the price of perpetual tenancy, will never have to pay any rent and Hwang Shang Sheng shall refrain from giving any cause for troubles. If there should be any question raised as to the anterior rights or ownership of the property or incumbrances thereon, he (Hwang Shang Sheng) shall undertake to settle it, which will not concern the tenant. It is also proper to declare that tax is payable upon the property. It being thought advisable to have evidence for the above this lease of perpetual tenancy is drawn up and handed over together with five old title deeds to be kept as proof.

(Signed) Woo Ut Ut, go-between. Hwang Kew Tik, witness.

(Signed) Hwang Shang Sheng, maker of lease of perpetual tenancy.

Lin Chang Yung, writer deputed.

Tung Chi, 5th year, 5th moon, 22nd day (1866).

Is that the deed you sent; it bears the Consular seal, you see? Yes, I see; as far as I remember that is correct—Well, it was not registered, was it? No.

Mr. Hayllar—And the Haukwan District Magistrate did not put his seal on it. Then I put that in, I shall have something to say about it presently. And eventually it resulted in your entering into the lease of 1876 for twenty years.

Re-examined by Mr. Hannen—Will you explain, please, as well as you can, the transaction with regard to those deeds which are mentioned in the petition as the false deeds which were given up; what was the nature of their falsehood? They had not the stamps of the Haukwan Magistrate on them; that was the only reason alleged for their falsehood by the authorities.—For how long did those deeds trace back the property? At this moment I really cannot say how far, but I should say for over a hundred years.—Was there a piece of land immediately alongside this piece, enclosed and occupied? At both sides of it.—Occupied by Chinese? Occupied by Chinese.—And still occupied by Chinese? Yes.

Mr. Hannen pointed out the piece of land referred to on the model and said it was a piece of Government property wedged in between two native houses.

At this stage the Court adjourned until the following day.

(Eighth Day, May 9th.)

Mr. Hannen continued his re-examination of the defendant.—Will you tell me whether the gate at the east end of the mission premises was put up in its present position in 1865, after that permission from the authorities? Yes.—Now with regard to the sale of the whole of that property, I mean the occasion when you sent triplicate deeds through the Consul to the city; did the priest tell you he had authority to sell? He did.—You told us you did not believe the priest had spent the money; is that so? Yes.—That was after the triplicate deeds came back? Yes.—Did you believe that if the priest ran away that promissory note would give you any title to the property? I did not.—Did you ever hear of a promissory note like that being registered at the Consulate? No.—Up to the deed of 1867, was it not the priest who had always received the rent for his own building? Yes, always.—Is that why you did not think the directors would be angry at his alienating it? Yes.—My learned friend made a great point, and indeed the whole petition does also, that the first attempted transaction was for the purchase of the whole of the property; have you any particular reasan by which you can remember it was for the Blind Man's Temple? Yes.—What is it? There is a note in the mission minute book about it.

Mr. Hannen tenders the minute referred to in evidence and says—It confirms his statement as to his negotiation for the purchase early in 1866 being for the Blind Man's Temple.

Mr. Hayllar—That you tried to purchase the Blind Man's Temple I have no doubt.

Mr. Hannen—Well, that is all I make of it.

His Lordship—The note I have is that "there is a note in the minute book which confirms my statement as to the negotiation early in 1866, being for the purchase of the Blind Man's Temple."

Mr. Hannen—Yes. The minute is dated 5th February, 1866, and is—

At a meeting of the Finance Committee, C. M. S., Foochow, held at the house of Rev. J. Wolfe, February 5th, 1866 (Tung Chi, 4th year, 12th moon, 25th day.)

Present Rev. J. R. Wolfe, Rev. A. W. Crible.

It was resolved—

(2)—That considering much damage has been done to the lower mission house (Rev. A. W. Crible's) by the inroads of the white ants coming in swarms from the adjoining Blind Man's Temple, and thereby causing considerable expense on the society from time to time for repairs, and also considering the great danger to the mission house in case fire should break out from the discharge of fire crackers during the tumultuous orgies at the said temple, steps should be at once taken with a view to the purchase of the temple for the society and if the attempt should prove successful that the old building should be pulled down and converted into a yard for the convenience of the lower mission house.

Mr. Hannen stated that the next witnesses he should call were Chinese and asked that the Rev.

Mr. Hartwell, of the American Board of Foreign Missions, should be sworn as interpreter.

Mr. Hayllar not objecting, Mr. Hartwell was sworn.

Wong Kin Taik, a Christian, said—I am a doctor. I first came to the premises occupied by the missionaries about the Taou Shan Kwan in 1863. I resided there for some time. I was living there in 1864. I have gone carefully over the premises recently, that is, between twenty and thirty days ago.

Mr. Hannen was going into the question of the position of the present wall as compared with the position of the old one, when Mr. Hayllar consented that for the purposes of this suit the statement of Mr. Wolfe with regard to the encroachment be taken as accurate.

The question as to whether the present dwelling house covered more or less ground than the old bungalow was also disposed of on the same basis, Mr. Hayllar stating that this was immaterial to his case, his contention being that the house occupied more land than was let; the old one might also have occupied more ground.

Evidence continued—When the present mission house was built I was living at a mission chapel in South-street, in the city, but was frequently at the new building. I never heard of any objection being made to the upper storey being put on the house. If any objection had been made to it I think I must have heard of it.

By Mr. Hayllar—When the mission house was burnt I do not remember there being a row about the east gate.

Ling Ayei Nei said—I am a mason. I knew the mission premises in Mr. Smith's time. I first knew them in 1859. I remember the place where the college now stands. That ground was enclosed, but the wall was low. I repaired the wall for Mr. Smith.

By Mr. Hayllar—It was a mud wall, only about eight or nine feet high. I have no books. I live at a place called Paun Yu San, outside the city. Since 1859 I have done no work at the premises. Mr. Wolfe invited me to come forward as a witness. When I was doing work for Mr. Smith he introduced me to Mr. Wolfe. Mr. Wolfe sent and called me in connection with this case. A man named Ka Siu came to me. He is Mr. Wolfe's cook. He is not a friend of mine. I have worked for Mr. Wolfe while Ka Siu has been Mr. Wolfe's cook. I have done work for Mr. Wolfe. I repaired a wall for him in 1866. It was the wall at the north-east. I have done no work since 1866. Ka Siu was Mr. Wolfe's cook at that time. He was not at the mission house when I repaired the wall in 1859, but there was a brother of his called Ka Kiu who was in the service. I came from my house to-day. I have been at Mr. Wolfe's house recently. Mr. Wolfe sent for me yesterday. I was there two days before and have gone whenever Mr. Wolfe has called me.

Mr. Hannen said he now proposed to call Mr. Stewart, chiefly to afford his learned friend an opportunity of cross-examining him.

Rev. R. W. Stewart, M.A., Trinity College, Dublin, said—I am a missionary of the Church Missionary Society. The new building which was burnt last year was built under my superintendence. I came to Foochow in November, 1876. The letter produced is the one I received from Mr. Sinclair in reference to the building of that college.

The letter, which was put in evidence, was as follows—

Dear Mr. Stewart,—I should have preferred waiting for the reply I am expecting from the Foreign Office to my dispatch concerning the exchange of houses, but as you desire so anxiously to begin operations I cease to have any objections to your doing so, but on one condition, which you will allow me to make, namely, that at the first symptom of opposition on the part of the gentry you at once discontinue the work of building. I hope sincerely you will go on quietly and that you will not be troubled.—Faithfully yours, Charles A. Sinclair.

Tuesday, April 2nd.

Examination continued—There was some opposition shown by the gentry afterwards. The building was completed as to the walls and roof and general exterior when that opposition came to my knowledge. This was a little over three months after I received Mr. Sinclair's letter. Mr. Sinclair then asked me to discontinue work on the house. I declined. Mr. Sinclair wrote to me to say the gentry were making objections and begging me to stop the work. I replied stating that the house was finished externally and there was nothing now for me to stop. Mr. Sinclair came and saw the house himself and said there was nothing now for him to do but to write and tell the authorities there was nothing to stop. Two days afterwards Mr. Sinclair wrote asking me to stop the work inside, which request I declined to accede to.

Mr. Hannen was putting a question as to what the witness considered the condition mentioned in Mr. Sinclair's first letter referred to.

Mr. Hayllar objected to the question and asked that Mr. Stewart's reply to Mr. Sinclair be produced.

Mr. Hannen said the letter was not in the defendant's possession.*

* The following is a copy of the letter referred to:—

Dear Mr. Sinclair,—Many thanks for your kind note. I make you the promise you ask, but hope very much there will be no need to fulfil it; indeed, I do not see what fault the gentry can find in our building a native-looking house on this particular spot, unseen, as it will be from the city.—Yours faithfully,

(Signed) Robert W. Stewart.

April 2nd, 1878.

Examination continued—I never undertook to stop the work pending a reference to the high authorities at home. I went yesterday and searched the records of the Consulate for correspondence relating to the period about 1865 and 1866. I searched the records from 1862 to 1867. From 1864 to 1866 there were no translations.

Mr. Hannen said he had intended to call Mr. Playfair, of the Consulate, to prove that there was no record of any such document as the deed of 1868 having been forwarded through the Consulate to the Chinese authorities.

Mr. Hayllar allowed this and said the case he made against the defendant was that that deed was never intended to go through the Consulate.

Mr. Hannen wished a note to be made of the fact.

Mr. Sinclair, recalled, said—With regard to informal notes, the substance is given to the writer, who afterwards brings the note for signature. The Consul, of course, reads it through. The substance of the note may be communicated to the writer through the interpreter. We keep no copy.

By Mr. Hayllar—I see the note of Mr. Carroll's. This is the form in which notes are sent. There is a date here; the witnesses said there was no date. The card has been pasted over it. The date is the 16th day of the 5th moon, but without any year being given. I know Mr. Carroll's signature very well, and it is subscribed to the document. The note follows a dispatch dated the 1st day of the 4th month of the 5th year of Tung Chi, so that the date of the note would probably be in June, 1866. The reference in my note to Mr. Stewart to the reply I was expecting from the Foreign Office was with regard to an offer made by Ting Futai, for exchange of the mission property at Wu Shih Shan for the telegraph property and $5,000 down. The telegraph property is on the island of Nantai, near Gilman and Co.'s private residence. The offer was made by Ting Futai through me to Mr. Wolfe. That was the negotiation referred to in that letter. I reported to the Foreign Office and to the Legation that the offer had been made and forwarded copies of my dispatches. At the time I wrote that letter I was expecting an answer from the Foreign Office. The letter was written on 2nd April, 1870, but the year is omitted. The tepao affixes his seal to documents relating to land. He does so after they are written. We require them at the Consulate for all leases in perpetuity. Leases without the tepao's seal are sent back. When a new magistrate comes fresh stamps are issued to the tepaos. I don't know whether that is for purposes of revenue; I imagine it may be. The revenue is collected with the assistance of the topao, who goes round with the tax-collector.

This concluded the evidence.

Mr. Hannen then summed up his case. He said—May it please your Lordship, I must begin by reiterating the objections which I raised to the petition before. Those objections, I hold, still stand. More than that, they are supplemented and enforced by the evidence which has been given for the defendant. It is not necessary for me to go through them again; your Lordship has a note of them and they will remain on the record for your Lordship to consider. I would now briefly point out, running through the petition, the points which appear to me to be important and which have not been made out, as I contend, by the plaintiff's case on evidence. The first thing that is to be observed is the 5th paragraph of the re-amended petition—"The above-mentioned two houses were Chinese built and were erected on land belonging to and formed part of the out buildings of the Taou Shan Kwan Temple. Having entered into possession thereof under the said agreement of rent the said lessees did subsequently, in breach of the terms and the true intent and meaning thereof and without the licence or authority of any one authorised in that behalf remove the said two houses and erect in their stead two structures of foreign design occupying sites considerably larger than those of the original buildings." This has not been proved and there is not one tittle of evidence to support it. Next, in the 6th paragraph it is said that the priest let the premises which were let to Messrs. Fearnley and Welton "without the consent or knowledge of any one authorised in that behalf." Now the whole course of the story tends to show that he was authorised in that behalf. Before 1867 the agreements were always made with the priest. Before that time the priest really was the agent of the directors for conducting the business, whatever it might be, concerned with the letting of the temple, and inasmuch as that lease was confirmed by the lease of 1867, supposing a jury were sitting here it would be right to direct the jury that there was evidence, from the fact of that confirmation of the lease of 1850, that there was authority in the priest to make the lease which is there set out. In that same paragraph, at the end, it is said "The said document was not recorded at the British Consulate, nor did it bear the said Consular seal, nor that of the Haukwan District Magistrate." It was expressly proved by the evidence of Ching Che Yeo, the Haukwan District Magistrate, that that is not necessary with regard to a lease of this kind in Chinese law and therefore the whole of the suggestion, whatever it may be, falls to the ground. Again, in the 7th paragraph, I have already pointed out, but I would again remind your Lordship, that the allegations there, that the missionaries "having entered into possession of the said rooms did, without reference to the said or to any local authorities, and without any licence or authority, and in breach of the intent and meaning of the said last mentioned agreement, alter and extend the said rooms by adding an upper storey and other rooms below," were not supported by any proof, at least as to extending them below, on the plaintiffs' part, and is expressly denied by the evidence which has been brought on behalf of the defendants. Again, in the 8th paragraph, it is said the lease to the Rev. George Smith was without any authority. With regard to that no evidence has been brought forward to show the priest had not authority, but, on the contrary, with regard to former leases the priest was the person dealt with. In the contract of 1850 he was expressly made a party and the validity of that lease has never been denied, and it is with the sanction of the Haukwan District Magistrate, so that the priest's authority to let under some circumstances really cannot be denied and has not been disproved. Here we have the first agreement made with the priest and the Haukwan District Magistrate being a party to it, the second agreement made with the priest, and afterwards the third agreement made with the priest and afterwards confirmed. There is therefore no ground for saying that up to 1867 the priest had no authority to let the premises. Now, I pass over the next paragraphs, because I must refer to them by and bye, and I come to the 19th paragraph, and there again is an allegation that in 1871, when the present house was being built, the defendant "encroached on land other than that leased to him and destroyed and removed a large rock." They have produced no evidence whatever to prove that the house now standing stands on a larger area than the old temples, and we have proved, and they have admitted, that the present house occupies less space than the old one, and they have not proved that the old one occupied any land belonging to the Taou Shan Kwan which was not leased. Now, with regard to the 20th paragraph. "In constructing a gateway and entrance road to the said house the defendant has interfered with and blocked up an ancient public right of way," they have not produced any evidence whatever to show that. Apparently the only way they intended to prove that was by cross-examining my witnesses, and they failed to prove it. That 20th paragraph is not supported by any evidence on the plaintiffs' side whatever. Then my lord, it really comes to this, that not one encroachment and not one breach of agreement has been proved.

Mr. Hayllar—Would you excuse my interrupting you to ask a question, do you say the land outside the walls is not ours?

Mr. Hannen—I say you have not proved that we have encroached on land belonging to you, and that we have not encroached on any other property than that which was let to us. Whether it belonged to you or not, and you wrongfully let it to us, we are not in a position to say. We suppose it did belong to you, as you let it. As far as your own case is concerned we say we have not encroached on any of the property which belongs to you.

Mr. Hayllar—Do you say that rock was let to you or not?

Mr. Hannen—Yes, we say it was. I shall come to that directly. At the present moment I merely wish to call your Lordship's attention to the fact that not one single encroachment or breach of agreement has been proved, and therefore the 25th paragraph falls to the ground; in fact, all the encroachments have been abandoned except the one with regard to this new house having been built upon land belonging to the temple which was not leased to the defendant, and I have proved distinctly that this house stood upon less ground than the old one. What was let to us was the old house.

His Lordship—Assuming the agreement of 1867 to be valid?

Mr. Hannen—Yes, my lord. We, therefore, have reduced the matter in reality to these three portions, the legal construction of the document, what was the vacant piece of ground, one of the parcels mentioned in the deed, and what was Mr. George Smith's piece of ground rented to him at $12 a year. That contains the whole gist of the petition as it now stands. It has been complicated by the story of the Taouist priest, which is a perfectly collateral state of things, and beyond what I have stated there is nothing in the petition now standing. There is simply—what is the construction of this agreement, what is the piece of land called the vacant piece of land, and what is Mr. George Smith's piece of land? It is true there is a question as to the rights of the parties under the lease of 1866, but with regard to that I propose passing it by. It is impossible for me to answer suddenly any construction my friend puts on that. If your Lordship thinks it necessary to put a construction upon this agreement and your Lordship makes any order we must be content to abide by it.

His Lordship—With regard to that agreement, I don't see how the plaintiffs have shown their right to any relief in regard to it. They have not alleged they have any right of property in respect of that land. That, I supposed, would be your point upon that agreement. As I understand it these directors sue as representing the temple.

Mr. Hayllar—Your Lordship is quite right.

Mr. Hannen—That is the construction I put upon it.

His Lordship—Well, then, they must show that they, as directors of the Taou Shan Kwan, have a right of suit upon the agreement of 1866. Is that shown on the petition?

Mr. Hannen—No, my lord.

His Lordship—Well, that is a point I should be disposed to ask Mr. Hayllar to address me upon. That seems to me to go to the gist of the whole.

Mr. Hannen—Yes, as to that.

Mr. Hayllar—Your Lordship sees they struck out the gentry as parties to the suit, but they did not strike out this paragraph.

His Lordship—Will you strike out the agreement of 1866 now?

Mr. Hayllar—No, my Lord, I am not going to strike it out now.

His Lordship—The question is whether the plaintiffs, as the pleadings now stand, have shown a right of suit under this agreement.

Mr. Hannen—But supposing that after hearing Mr. Hayllar your Lordship should hold they had, I cannot argue upon the rights of the parties under the deed, because no specific ambiguity, breach, or anything else is alleged. I come to the trial of this case without knowing in the least what my learned friend is going to allege about it.

His Lordship—They have not proved the agreement of 1866.

Mr. Hayllar—It is admitted in the answer.

Mr. Hannen—Practically it is admitted. At the time of drawing up the answer to the petition we could not admit the accuracy of the translation, and at the present moment I have no reason for challenging its accuracy.

His Lordship—There has been no ambiguity alleged except at the bar, and Mr. Hayllar's argument is, supposing Mr. Wolfe goes way or becomes defunct, who are "the others" to whom he is to look. He is looking for something and he finds a shadow

Mr. Hayllar—Yes, my lord, and he has made an agreement not to sublet.

Mr. Hannen—It really is, as I imagine, a lease to Mr. Wolfe in trust for himself and others connected with the Church Mission. However, I decline to bind myself with regard to that I say I cannot answer it, because I have not been put in a position to do so—at least, I ought not to be put in that position, because the plaintiffs have not shown their interest.

His Lordship—That is what I say.

Mr. Hannen—Nor have they shown it in the course of the case. Well, I pass from these objections to the petition and proof to what still remains. I say, therefore, now, that we really are brought face to face with the three points, what is the construction of the document, what was the piece of land mentioned in paragraph 16, and what was the piece of land leased to Mr. Smith?

Mr. Hayllar—Allow me to call your attention to the word "local authorities" which you use in the 14th paragraph of the answer—"I admit that, as stated in the 14th paragraph of the amended petition, an agreement to rent some land for building purposes close to the Wan Chang Kung Temple was, in or about the month of September, 1866, entered into between myself and others of the English Church Missionary Society and the local authorities." Is that so or is it not? We are "local authorities"—very local.

Mr. Hannen—It is only an acknowledgment of the agreement The authorities we allude to are the authorities mentioned in the agreement.

Mr. Hayllar—And you didn't make your agreement with them.

Mr. Hannen—We say it is.

Mr. Hayllar—The Government?

Mr. Hannen—Apparently it was the Government, and the gentry, and all united together. Now, I am obliged, before entering on the legal construction of the agreement of 1867, to allude once more to this story of the priest and his three documents and Mr. Wolfe's reply to it. Mr. Hayllar attempted to puzzle Mr. Wolfe by the introduction of that note from Mr. Carroll. It did not in the least shake Mr. Wolfe's distinct impression as to what was the truth of the matter. Although, no doubt, that note as placed in his hands was on the face of it difficult to explain, and although Mr. Wolfe had an opportunity of reconsidering what he said, he still adhered, and adheres still, to the statement he made that the priest was imprisoned on account of the first transaction and not on account of the second, and although fifty people were to try to place documents in his hand and divert his attention from that fact, he still maintains that it was with regard to the first transaction and not with regard to the second. Now, the whole gist of Mr. Hayllar's cross-examination on that point was that having looked at Mr. Carroll's letter on that point Mr. Wolfe ought to say he was mistaken because Mr. Carroll's letter speaks of the lease of the whole of the ground occupied by Mr. Wolfe. But let us see what that letter was. That letter was an unofficial note. The way in which an unofficial note is drawn up was detailed to us this morning by Mr. Sinclair. The Consul tells shortly, possibly through the interpreter, to the writer what he is to say and the writer draws up what the letter is. Now, inasmuch as there had been at that time, no doubt, a complaint made about the attempt to sell the Blind Man's Temple, no doubt that had come to the knowledge of Mr. Carroll through the authorities. Then comes the question of the priest being imprisoned. It has never been said that anything definite was brought to the knowledge of the Consul. It is not said on the other side that Mr. Wolfe passed these documents through the Consular books in order to go to the authorities; therefore the Consul had nothing but a verbal report of some kind as to what took place, the main gist of which was that a perpetual lease of some kind had been attempted to be obtained by Mr. Wolfe and had failed. That being so, the writer seems to have assumed this related to the whole of the premises, whereas it related only to the Blind Man's Temple. And in an unofficial note, drafted in this loose way, this mention is made, and then the whole of Mr. Wolfe's credit is to be shaken—although he swears most strongly what the transaction was —by the writer having put in words which my learned friend contends show that the transaction had taken place with regard to the whole of the property instead of the Blind Man's Temple only! Now I think that is very unfair. He is here on his oath, he knows his responsibility and the penalty for not speaking the truth far better than can be known by the witnesses on the other side. The penalty for perjury is far greater, as applied to a person in his position, both in its moral condemnation and actual punishment, than is inflicted, if any is inflicted, on Chinese. A loose note, which may have been written through a double interpretation, is produced, and that it should be suggested Mr. Wolfe's testimony is untrue, because it didn't agree with that which appears to be in that note, is unfair. Now, there is also the $800 deed to be accounted for. That deed is accounted for at first by my learned friend in this way, he says that was drawn up by Mr. Wolfe, was handed to the priest for his signature, was handed back to Mr. Wolfe, and when I objected to its production he says "I have traced it into your possession." He has, but how does he trace it out? The only way would be through the Consulate. But then we should have had a note in the Consular books to that effect, and we have shown, and my learned friend has admitted, there is no such note. Therefore he has traced the note into Mr. Wolfe's hands and he leaves it there, and yet it turns up in the archives of a Chinese yamên. Then, again, a very grave charge is attempted to be rested by Mr. Hayllar on that. The charge which is made, which on the testimony of the priest alone would have very little chance of being believed, is corroborated by a document the appearance of which among the Chinese archives was never accounted for. It is simply placed baldly before the witness, and not one single word of proof is given as to how it came there. Now upon these documents rested another thing, the fact that there was an attempt to purchase something, which failed, and then, shortly afterwards, an attempt to purchase something and a payment of money on account, and my learned friend laid great stress in his cross-examination upon that —that although the first attempt had failed yet Mr. Wolfe was willing to pay $500 on account of the second. But Mr. Wolfe's account makes that perfectly clear. He says the first was an attempt to buy the Blind Man's Temple. That was perfectly fresh property. He attempted to extend his premises then and failed, but that was no reason why he should think the directors would be unwilling to sell what he was already occupying. What he was already occupying had been changed by other people from the original estate, and it might well be the directors would be willing to sell him that although they would not be willing to sell him fresh property, more especially as he was under the impression he held under a lease which gave him power to hold as long as he liked. The effect of the priest having attempted to sell and failed on the first occasion would only make Mr. Wolfe think when he came again and said, "Now I have authority to sell"—what would pass through his mind would be, "I suppose he really has got the authority of the directors this time," so it is far less likely he would imagine there was any doubt as to the success of the second transaction than that there would be as to the first, more especially as the property was actually in his possession, whereas what he attempted to purchase before was a temple and was not in his possession. Now, there is another point which my learned friend alluded to, perhaps only by a sneer—the fact that Mr. Wolfe and Mr. Smith had in their possession what are called false deeds. With regard to this the reason the deeds came into their possession is very clear. The first preliminaries as to the purchase of little bits of ground are simply these: you get the deeds from the owner, they are sent to the tepao, and they are then sent to the Consulate. With regard to that we hear that Mr. Smith died suddenly and his papers were left in confusion, and these deeds which he had got, and which he probably would have passed through the regular channel and got stamped, were not stamped, and Mr. Wolfe, who had only been here a little time, did not know the importance of it.

Mr. Hayllar—We had no evidence of that.

Mr. Hannen—He has said himself that he came in 1862 and this was in 1863, and he states he had not had the management of the property. The whole thing being in confusion it is not at all extraordinary he did not take the procaution which he ought to have done of having these deeds passed through the regular channel. Now there is only one incidental point I want to touch upon, and that is as to my having objected to the documents. My learned friend will make a great deal of that. It only amounts to this, that not knowing their effect if they were in evidence, I preferred they should not be introduced into the case. I have never had any chance of seeing them before, and most of them refer to a time during which no English translations were kept in the Consulate. I had therefore had no opportunity of seeing them, they came upon me perfectly fresh, and with regard to the greater portion of them I thought it prudent, as I had not had time to consider them, not to admit them. Mr. Stewart has shown that between 1864 and nearly the end of 1866, during the time Mr. Sinclair was absent, there is a hiatus of translations in the consular records. That accounts fully, I maintain, for the objections I have made, and my friend must take all the advantage he can. I am, of course, bound by what I have done and the course I have taken. Now, the next point we come to is the lot of ground mentioned in the agreement of 1867, "A small piece of land formerly hired under a verbal agreement by the Missionary George Smith." When we point out that this is the piece of land on which the college stands, my learned friend says it could not be that because the directors had no right to let it.

Mr. Hayllar—Excuse me, you have not given one word of evidence on the subject.

Mr. Hannen—We have given Mr. Wolfe's evidence that he believed this was the piece, and you have no more.

Mr. Hayllar—We have the priest who let it.

Mr. Hannen—Well, he comes and tells us he let this piece (pointing it out on the map) at $12, while he let this other piece with the house on it at $20. The thing is ridiculous. This was done before our time. It was simply impossible for us to have any direct testimony of what was let to Mr. Smith; all we know is what appeared to be let to us in the agreement of 1867. One of my learned friend's arguments is that the directors had no power to let it, but when they come to point out what they did let they point out a piece which, according to their own showing, they had no right to let.

Mr. Hayllar—The directors did not; Chun Yuen Ching did.

Mr. Hannen—The two together show they had let a piece of ground not within the walls. If they did that than there is no more reason why they should not let this piece of land than there is for imagining they let the piece they say they did. At the time Mr. Wolfe made the agreement of 1867 the only piece of waste ground was the piece at the back of the house and that represented in Mr. Wolfe's mind the piece of vacant ground referred to in the first part of the agreement. If the directors, who were constantly at the Taou Shan Kwan, drew up in the deliberate way in which they did this lease, it seems extraordinary they should go and speak of a house with so many rooms with a piece of vacant ground, when in reality they say that piece of ground did not exist. It was only natural on Mr. Wolfe's part to believe they intended to rent to him the piece of vacant ground which was and is attached to the house. It is a very extraordinary thing indeed if these directors actually go and describe what is a house having no vacant ground as a house with a vacant piece of ground; if it had been their intention to have let a house attached to which there was no vacant ground they would not have said there was any. Under the circumstances it does not seem to me so very extraordinary that Mr. Wolfe should have taken that to be the land and have used it accordingly. I say they have to prove as an affirmative fact that that is not the piece of ground and they have not proved affirmatively what is the piece. We, having acted in perfectly good faith, are not to be held blameable for it. They tell us they have let us a piece of vacant ground. We imagine we have got it and use it, and if your Lordship tells us that is not the piece we give it up willingly. We imagined this was it, and we certainly would not have entered into this agreement, which we believed was to include everything within the walls, if we had known it was not.

His Lordship—There is nothing in the least to show that you were to have everything within the walls.

Mr. Hannen—No; there is not; but what Mr. Wolfe understood was that he was to have one single document representing the whole of the ground within the walls. It does not seem an improbable story, at least, that when he is in occupation of this property and a fresh lease is to be made, it should be intended to include all he was in possession of, and it has never been disputed for ten years. He has been in possession for ten years without any dispute, and it has never been disputed until other outside questions were imported into it.

Mr. Hayllar—Until you attempted to build on it, which was the only way in which it could come into dispute.

Mr. Hannen—But they have not said they did not know it was used before. Are these gentlemen who come to the temple twice a month to be supposed not to know we were in occupation? For ten years you don't say a word against it until something quite different from the present point I am upon—whether it was leased at all or not—arises. For ten years you go on taking our rent without saying we are occupying land we ought not to.

His Lordship—You were on the land.

Mr. Hayllar—They were squatters on Government ground.

His Lordship—They were enclosed squatters.

Mr. Hannen—And the land had been enclosed for twenty years.

Mr. Hayllar—Yes, according to the cook's friend.

Mr. Hannen—We have proved distinctly it has been enclosed since 1862, the time of Mr. Wolfe's arrival. He swears it was enclosed then, and my learned friend admitted it. Well then, according to Mr. Wolfe's account and according to the mason's account, that ground has been enclosed, for twenty years according to the mason, since 1862 according to Mr. Wolfe, and we have been in occupation for ten years and more without any objection having been made. Now, of course, in what I have to say with regard to the buildings upon that piece of land I assume, as I believe it to be true and as I believe my case has made it out to be, that that land was leased to us by the agreement of 1867. With regard to that, it is for my learned friend to make out that building upon a piece of ground of that sort is not allowed, first of all, and as he has even spoken of taking advantage of the forfeiture if he proved it to be theirs, he has also to prove that building upon a piece of land of this sort works a forfeiture. Now, I must say a word as to how it came to be built upon. It was built upon because they thought they had a right, and Mr. Sinclair thought so at the time, or at any rate, that he did not think to the contrary is shown by his note in which he withdraws his objection. He thinks it inexpedient, but at that time there was a *bonâ fide* belief that they were entitled to build. That being so, supposing us not to have a right, no penalty ought to be inflicted on us for doing what we believed we had a right to do, and what was done in a perfectly *bonâ fide* spirit. I say that, supposing there is a custom of forfeiture. But my learned friend has to prove that, and he has not done so. The only evidence he has on the subject was that he asked the ex-Prefect Ting whether, under an agreement of this kind, a building could be placed on ground like this. That may be, but it does not follow that it works a forfeiture. Now there is another reason why, even supposing it to be an unauthorised and unlawful act, it ought not to work a forfeiture, and that is this very broad one, a principle which permeates every law and which is a law of reason as well as the law of England, and that is that when in an agreement of this kind one thing is expressed then what is not expressed is understood. Here it says that the rent is not to get into arrears; should this happen the directors may resume and or let the place to somebody else. Under these circumstances, they having expressed a ground of forfeiture, that is the only one which can be allowed to work; the expression of that shows it was the only ground of forfeiture and no other ground can be imported into it. With regard to the construction we put upon this document, we must say now, although I think under the petition we ought not to be called upon to do so, yet we have to say what construction we put upon that lease. We say it is a lease to us for so long as we pay rent.

His Lordship—That is, assuming the lease to be valid?

Mr. Hannen—Yes.

His Lordship—You say that is expressed?

Mr. Hannen—Yes. If you read that document by the light of common sense and nothing else you come to the conclusion it is a lease to us for so long as we pay rent.

His Lordship—You would not call it a lease in perpetuity?

Mr. Hannen—No.

His Lordship—Because you might throw it up.

Mr. Hannen—We might throw it up. And there is nothing repugnant to reason in such a lease, and nothing repugnant to the law of China so far as it has been shown to us, or even in a perpetual lease, because they have made perpetual leases of the ground which has been transferred to foreigners throughout the country. But this perpetual lease has been invented by them, and therefore it is only reasonable to suppose it is not contrary to their views of what may be taken. If then a perpetual lease can be taken, *a fortiori*, a lease for so long as a person pays rent cannot be repugnant. Now, I say the only construction of this document is, as I put it, a lease for so long as we pay rent. My learned friend, on the other hand, puts a perfectly forced construction upon it, and bases that upon what he says is the law of China. The evidence of that, my Lord, I venture to submit is very weak. It is the evidence given by two persons, Ting, the former Prefect, and the present Hankwan Magistrate. These two gentlemen contradicted each other flatly as to the law and custom with regard to leases. The one said that a lease between landlord and tenant was drawn up in duplicate, it was signed by both of them, and each held a copy. The other said, what is the fact, that the lease is drawn up by the tenant and handed to the landlord, and that is no doubt because *prima facie* the person in possession of the land is the person who would be taken to be the owner, and when that is not the case he hands a document to the landlord as proof of this. That, I believe, is the correct form of the lease, but, whatever it is, these two gentlemen directly contradicted themselves. Therefore I say it is not very strong evidence as to what the law of the place is, when the only witnesses called to prove it contradict each other flatly. Now, there is more than that. Both these gentlemen admit this is a case entirely beyond their comprehension and ordinary practice. Their evidence is that before foreigners came to China temple lands were never let at all; therefore it is impossible they should know the form of agreement when temple lands are let. They say the ordinary custom is that a landlord can resume either to live in the house himself or let it to his son. But such cases as that do not apply to temple lands and the circumstances of the present case, and therefore they cannot be made here to force a construction of the document which the document on its face does not bear. It is perfectly distinct on the face of it what it means, and if you import into it what is the custom with regard to shops and ordinary houses, you get into what my friend called shifting sands and have no solid ground. We want to follow simply the deed and not to have imported any custom which is not certain, as shown by the persons called to prove it. We want simply to go upon the deed according to what it means on the face of it. But there is always this contention underlying my friend's argument, that the main reason why we should not interpret this to be a lease of this kind is that the directors could not make such a lease and therefore could not intend to make it. We have had no direct evidence as to that, but my learned friend entered into an exceedingly interesting description of what these societies were, in order to prove it was not likely they would be able to let temple lands. But what they are and what they profess to do has nothing to do with the matter. They are societies whose directors assumed to deal with these lands and whom we assume had the right to do so, and there is no intrinsic reason why, because a society occupies itself with the supplying of lamps and incense to the temple, it should not in common with others let the land. The directors may well be the directors of an association which nominally does this, but which really, in common with the others, has the management of these lands. They say they are called together, and meet, and make arrangements, and so on, and why should we believe, merely on my learned friend's *exposé* of the nature of these societies, that they have not this power? They tell us they did draw this lease up in solemn form, and then my learned friend wants to make us believe it was to make a lease which might be upset at the end of three months, and which by the evidence of the Haukwan Magistrate, would terminate without any warning. By his evidence, if the landlord refuses to receive the rent, out the tenant must go without any warning whatever. They took such care to frame it in the way they did, and all this in order to draw up a lease which was only to have effect for three months! I venture to think that is preposterous, and that they intended it to have a very much longer effect than three months, and that in fact it was to give a tenancy which did last undisputed for ten years and was to last as long as the rent was paid. My learned friend's contention is that during the whole of that time the directors, and people, and everyone, were opposed to the residence of the missionaries there.

His Lordship—And they gave you a lease in 1866?

Mr. Hannen—Yes. My learned friend says it was merely to give us a licence, but they allowed us to reside for ten years under this licence without once attempting to eject us under what everybody knows to be a custom, although all the time they were grumbling at our residence. The agreement of 1867 says "On the other hand, if the rent does not get into arrears the place may not be let to any one else. Both parties being of the same mind neither of them can withdraw." What, then, is the meaning of neither of them being able to withdraw, if one party can withdraw at the end of three months; I don't understand. My learned friend's contention is that the lessors can withdraw at the end of three months and leave the lessees to scramble out of the place as quickly as they can. These seem to me to be very important words to get over. Your Lordship will also observe that in the agreement of 1866, towards the end, it says "At the expiration of the said term, if before the departure of the tenants for their native country, China should require the said ground for her own use, one month's previous notice to that effect will be given to the tenants who will then give up possession of it without the least hindrance." My contention is that when it is intended by the landlord to resume possession without the consent of the tenant these are the sort of words that are used. "If China should require the said ground for her own use;" it is paraphrasing what would be said if it was an ordinary landlord, "If the landlord should require the said land," etc. Supposing it to be the law of China that a landlord can at any time eject a tenant at the end of three months, or one month as the District Magistrate said, what would be the object of putting in an express provision in this deed that if China should require the land she can take it by giving one month's notice. If my learned friend's contention is correct, China would be able to resume without this clause. But that is the sort of deed drawn up between Chinese when they intend the landlord shall be entitled to resume, and if they had intended that here, in the lease of 1867, they would have put in an express clause that at the end of three months the landlord might resume for his own use. That not being so, the landlord cannot resume.

His Lordship—You see, with reference to the agreement of 1866, you are the tenant for twenty years; then you may be turned out at the expiration of the twenty years upon one month's notice; that is to say, if they give you one month's notice at the end of nineteen years and eleven months you have to go at the end of the twenty years.

Mr. Hannen—It contemplates something else. It says "at the expiration of the said term, if before the departure of the tenants for their native country, China should require the ground for her own use, one month's previous notice to that effect will be given to the tenants who will then give up possession of it without the least hindrance." There they expressly put in the clause which is the general way of doing it in ordinary leases between Chinese. Reading these two documents, and reading the one which more nearly corresponds to the documents between Chinese, I say there is a deed having this clause in, and if it is the law that they can do it without why should they put it in? And I draw from that the inference that it should be put in, if it is intended the landlord should resume.

Mr. Hayllar—There is the strongest evidence that agreements for terms of years are unknown in China, they are only given for the benefit of foreigners.

Mr. Hannen—It is also to be observed, with regard to the point I was mentioning just now, that although the authorities and people have always been restive under the residence of the missionaries there, yet they did not for ten years try the procedure of giving notice or refusing the rent, but we have it in evidence from Mr. Sinclair that in order to get rid of the missionaries from that place they offered a very large and handsome compensation. Now, is it to be believed that if they could have got rid of them by one stroke of the pen they would give this compensation? If they had known this was the law would they not there and then have given the notice?

His Lordship—I think, from my present experience, they would have been very glad to have got rid of all these proceedings.

Mr. Hayllar—My lord, rather than have had this suit China would have paid $50,000.

Mr. Hannen—That is hardly a matter of evidence. Now, my lord, almost the last thing I wish to point out is that according to their own view of the matter, although the plaintiffs could resume, they could not, according to the strict words of this agreement, let the place to any body else. Now, as to that, how is your Lordship and this court going to bind the plaintiffs. They may, the moment they have got rid of us, let it to somebody else, and your Lordship will have no control over them whatever. I think a court of equity will be very slow to make a decree over which it has no control so far as one of the parties is concerned.

Mr. Hayllar—Well, my Lord, I will give a bond with the highest possible penalty and the defendant can sue upon it.

Mr. Hannen—My learned friend has taught me the old style of pleading has not gone out so much as I hoped it had. I thought the time of interrupting counsel and bullying witnesses had gone by.

Mr. Hayllar—Did I bully witnesses?

Mr. Hannen, in reply, referred to Mr. Hayllar's cross-examination of the defendant. He then, addressing the court, said he thought he had gone through the whole of the case so far as it was necessary.

His Lordship—Have you gone through the whole of the law?

Mr. Hannen—I think I have.

His Lordship—There is one point I think myself bound to call your attention to. Mr. Hayllar's argument is, and he put it in the very front, that the lease is void.

Mr. Hannen—But he has not proved that. He says the lease is void on the ground that the directors had no right to make it.

His Lordship—No, that there was no commencement.

Mr. Hannen—That the directors had no right to make it.

His Lordship—No; assuming they had a perfectly valid title, assuming this was a lease of land under the Duke of Devonshire, the lease is void because no commencement is stated in the lease. Then again comes in the question, if the lease is void, what then? It is out of the way. I don't think you can overlook the point, because it is a very important one. I have not had an opportunity of looking into the cases referred to in support of Mr. Hayllar's position, namely, that the commencement of a lease as well as the termination must be asserted. Now, here Mr. Hayllar's point is that there is no commencement. Suppose you did not pay rent and action was brought, your answer would be, when does the rent commence? Is that not what you say?

Mr. Hayllar—Yes.

Mr. Hannen—That would be no answer.

His Lordship—Certainly it would be an answer. Suppose you had not entered into possession?

Mr. Hannen—But we had entered into possession, and that makes all the difference, my lord.

His Lordship—The question is, whether it does make any difference.

Mr. Hannen—According to English law I cannot pretend this lease would be valid.

His Lordship—You cannot say it, but it is a point I must consider. You see we have got to look to English law and we have got to look to Chinese law, but supposing I feel myself compelled on the very threshold of the case to decide this point in the plaintiffs' favour I need not go any further. Mr. Hayllar might have had books here which would have settled the point at once. If he had it would have saved a good deal of trouble. It may be these cases are conclusive on the point. There is no doubt you are in possession, and therefore it is I should like to see what these cases say. Well, then there is this, supposing the lease is void then there is no lease whatever and you would come under your former documents. Would that not be so?

Mr. Hayllar—No. my lord, that would not be so; we have got them.

His Lordship—Have you surrendered your former documents?

Mr. Hannen—Yes; I have never contended that.

His Lordship—But you have not considered that point, or not advanced it in argument.

Mr. Hannen—No; what I say is, first of all, with regard to this lease, we have parted with the documents we held before. That is a fact we cannot get over.

His Lordship—Have you made what in English law would be considered a surrender of your previous lease?

Mr. Hannen—Yes, we have. My Lord, this is the very reason why at the very threshold I objected to going into these questions. I said at the beginning that my learned friend ought to have alleged what he was going to say about these two leases, that it was void for a particular reason. whereas I come down here—we are entirely away from our books—and I don't know what he is going to contend.

His Lordship—He has stated at the bar.

Mr. Hannen—But I have not had time to send to Shanghai for my books.

His Lordship—I shall not give judgment at the conclusion of the argument; I must look at the authorities.

Mr. Hannen—I am saying this partly to strengthen my previous objection and also to excuse myself for not assisting your Lordship so m as I otherwise should have been able to douch

His Lordship—Well, that is a point I must look to, and as to what would be the effect of l ease void I have nothing to do with. I shall consider myself bound to consider what Mr. Hayllar stated, namely, that the commencement of a lease must be asserted as well as the termination, but as matters stand we have only to do with the commencement; there is no commencement stated.

Mr. Hannen—It is an agreement made on a particular day to do a particular thing.

His Lordship—No, there is no date, it is not stated when the term is to commence.

Mr. Hannen—It is true it is not dated on a day, but it dated in the month of August.

His Lordship—But there is no statement in the body of the lease of the term which is to be the commencement of the lease. As I said to you, suppose these Chinese people had tried to fasten you with rent, suppose you had not taken possession and they had gone to Mr. Sinclair and filed a petition in his Court for the payment of the rent, where would they have been? Why, the whole thing would have been nowhere.

Mr. Hannen—The whole aspect of the matter is changed by entry.

His Lordship—Well, that is your argument.

Mr. Hannen—Yes.

His Lordship—Of course, but I mean to say I cannot decide the point merely upon argument. It is a point I have not lost sight of and therefore I thought it as well to draw your attention to it before you sat down.

Mr. Hannen—My argument is that in a lease of real property of this kind the strict rules of English law cannot be imported, and I believe it is my friend's case, too. The question arose some time ago and the opinion of the law officers of the Crown was asked. That was published in the *Hongkong Government Gazette*. and it is the old rule that the *lex loci rei sitæ* prevails; I mean that the English laws as to real property ought not to be imported into questions of real property here.—The learned counsel then read the opinion referred to, published in the *Hongkong Government Gazette* in the year 1856. It was to the effect that such cases ought to be decided according to the *lex loci* where it could be ascertained, and where it could not, according to the principles of natural justice.

His Lordship—How do you apply this to the present case? I am merely drawing your attention to Mr. Hayllar's argument. Do you say this opinion answers that?

Mr. Hannen—I think it applies. There is nothing extraordinary or ambiguous about this lease in reality. Here is a document dated and drawn up, etc. I say that if the rule of common justice is applied it must mean what I say.

His Lordship—Well, let us apply the rule of common justice. you are not obliged to enter?

Mr. Hannen—Then I don't think I ought to be made to pay rent.

His Lordship—But here is your contract; if it had said you entered on the 1st August you would be bound?

Mr. Hannen—Why, then of course we would be bound to pay it.

His Lordship—Well, then, suppose under this agreement you had not entered and the plaintiffs had brought an action against you, would you have paid the rent in court?

Mr. Hayllar—My Lord, why should I take into consideration in a case ——

His Lordship—Oh, if you decline to answer it there is an end of it. It is a very common thing to put cases to counsel in argument. Well, now, I say, how would the plaintiffs here have been able to fix upon any time from which the payment of rent was to commence? If it had stated the 1st August you said you would have been liable. How would you say the Court ought to determine the rent if you did not enter into possession?

Mr. Hannen—The date itself not being mentioned, if they could fix the date by internal evidence they would then be entitled to rent according to what the law officers of the Crown call the common rules of justice.

His Lordship—They might be able to show *aliende*, by something *dehors* the agreement, from what term. But the case I am putting is not entering into possession, and also what Mr. Hayllar was saying the other day about the necessity of having a commencement stated.

Mr. Hannen—Well, that is what I say is one of the rules that was intended to be excluded by the law officers of the Crown.

His Lordship—But have you shown me that in anything I say there is anything that runs counter to the law of China?

Mr. Hannen—I say the law of China has not been ascertained, and therefore the rules of common justice must be applied.

His Lordship—And that where the law of England is express it is to be thrown over and the rules of common justice applied, which vary according to the measure of the foot of the man who happens to preside in Court.

Mr. Hannen—I must again apologise for not having been able to render more assistance to your Lordship on this point. I have looked through everything that has come within my ken and have laid all the argument before you I have been able to do. I am very sorry, for your Lordship and my client, that I have not been able to do more, but your Lordship understands my position.

His Lordship—Certainly.

The Court adjourned until the following day.

(Ninth Day, May 10th.)

Mr. Hannen said he found his clients, on looking at their documents, had discovered the old lease of 1850. He was under the impression it had been given up, but it had not, and there it was.

Mr. Hayllar said the Chinese authorities had had the lease in question returned to them in an official form by Mr. Sinclair, as he was able to prove.

Mr. Hannen said there might have been more than one copy.

After some discussion Mr. Hayllar consented to the document being received in evidence *quantum valeat*.

His Lordship said that in this case he could not pronounce any opinion as to the effect of the old document; he had merely suggested to Mr. Hannen that in case the lease of 1867 were invalid, the old one might revive.

Mr. Hannen referred his Lordship to several cases bearing upon points at issue in the present case, and also put in evidence receipts for rent given to the plaintiffs, signed by the Board of Trade, the last of which was dated the 9th October and was for the quarter ending 31st December, 1878.

Mr. Hayllar then replied. He said—May it please you my Lord, there are three or four points to which I would just call your Lordship's attention to begin with. The first is, why did my learned friend, with that opinion before him, which I understand he put in last night, try to keep out my foreign law, my evidence on Chinese law?

Mr. Hannen—On the ground which I stated, that it ought to have been alleged in the petition.

His Lordship—I don't think Mr. Hannen went so far as to say no evidence ought to be received, but he said you have not alleged and therefore you ought not to prove.

Mr. Hayllar—Yes, that is so, but I am going to found one or two remarks upon it. Now, my Lord, upon that there is nothing more clear, I apprehend, in the English law than that foreign law, the *lex loci rei sitæ* must govern this case. Your Lordship asked me yesterday to bring in Forsyth's Opinions, and here is a perfect cloud of authorities. The learned counsel quoted a passage from Forsyth, and proceeded—that being so, the case, I put it, really lies in a complete nutshell. If I had had the remotest conception of the course which my learned friend was going to take, if I had had the slightest idea that my evidence on Chinese law, which I tendered to your Lordship and which you will find—and this is a point I could not offer evidence upon, but it is a matter of common knowledge—comes from the only source from which such evidence can be obtained, namely, those who administer the law in China—if I had known this evidence was to remain uncontradicted in any way, I would not have troubled your Lordship at such length

I shall have a word or two to say about custom, but if my learned friend had no evidence to contradict that, I cannot understand why he is here.

His Lordship—Or why a special case could not have been submitted to the court.

Mr. Hannen—If they had chosen to do that we might have agreed to it.

Mr. Hayllar—If I had had the slightest idea of what the line taken by my learned friend was going to be, I certainly should not have troubled myself with what has been the main portion of my case, namely, corroborative testimony. Your Lordship sees, my position was this—I had expected, as it turns out wrongly, that my learned friend would contend that the law and custom were not in favour of that document, and I saw a great many gentlemen here whom I thought were going to give evidence on that point. However, they were not called and I took an immense amount of pains, and I took up a great deal of your Lordship's time, in an attempt to show, and I think to successfully show, that the state of the law, as I alleged it to be, was in the minds and knowledge of the parties when they made that agreement of 1867. That it was in the minds of the Chinese parties must now be obvious to everyone, for this reason, that as we had taken an infinity of pains to prevent this gentleman getting by direct means a permanent location on this site, we were certainly not by a side wind going to give him what we had refused to give him directly, and more especially so as we were at the time particularly incensed with him. That is so far as the Chinese are concerned. What Mr. Wolfe's knowledge of the law of China was on that particular point of course I don't know, but he was a gentleman upon his own showing very active in seeking and getting property, and he had a Chinese teacher by him, and it is not likely he approached this important subject in complete innocence of the law bearing upon it. I don't know that the two former documents, the one of 1850 and the one of 1855, throw much light upon his acts, because Mr. Wolfe must have known enough of the position of his society and of his relation with that society, and clearly of his relations with those gentlemen whom Mr. Hannen has alluded to in his speech as his predecessors, to know perfectly well that documents made between the Chinese priest and Messrs. Welton and Fearnley would not enure to his benefit, could not possibly do so by any means, and that therefore he clearly held the property under a yearly agreement. That is what Mr. Wolfe must have known. But Mr. Wolfe had received in the course of these transactions one or two lessons on the law. He had found in the first instance, according to his own statement, that it was impossible to buy the Blind Man's Temple out and out. He had found that it was impossible for him to get the property he held, which he attempted to purchase, possibly, as he says, for $1,500, certainly, as I say, for $500. He had then, as we say, gone a circuitous course still to get hold of the property in a sort of permanent way. He puts it that the vital interest of getting back $500 led him to the situation in which he made this contract called the promissory note. I put it on the evidence of the priest that he did it deliberately, and I think I shall show your Lordship presently the completest proof that the story of the priest is the real truth of the transaction. But Mr. Wolfe had found out that that did not succeed, that in opint of fact it raised a tremendous storm, and he then received from the directors of the temple a document headed in the English language "agreement of rent," which, as your Lordship recollects, is not recorded at the Consulate, and was not, from its very nature, intended to have a permanent effect. He received that document and under the circumstances he must have drawn the inevitable conclusion that it gave him nothing more than a tenancy from year to year. Now, Mr. Wolfe is a gentleman who, according to his own admission, goes backwards and forwards to the Consulate pretty frequently. We know of a despatch which has been referred to by Mr. Consul Sinclair, which my friend called Mr. Sinclair's evidence about, and we know what that despatch says about an annual tenancy, and how could Mr. Carroll when he wrote it know anything about this matter except from Mr. Wolfe? How comes Mr. Consul Carroll to refer to an annual tenancy in his despatch? My Lord, it could only have been though Mr. Wolfe being very considerably alarmed at wha had happened to the priest—whether the priest had been taken into custody for the $400 or $500 the alarm would be the same. He must have felt his position was pretty perilous, and he must have asked the assistance of the Consul about it. Therefore, certainly at that period what Mr. Wolfe was trying to get in a legitimate way was an annual tenancy, and when after that he entered into that transaction about the promissory note, that slippery transaction as I call it, he must have known perfectly well that it could only be carried through by a trick and that all he could hope to obtain from the Chinese authorities through the proper channel was a tenancy from year to year. Now, my Lord, these are my two pieces of corroborative testimony, that the Chinese would never have given indirectly what they would not give directly, what they struggled against, and that Mr. Wolfe himself must have acted on that understanding. My learned friend shut out all evidence of custom by his objections. I should have been glad to have tried the case, so far as this went, on a much more open basis than it at present stands on. I should have been glad to have called a great many more witnesses on the subject of the custom, and I should have been very glad of any evidence of Mr. Wolfe himself in contradiction if it had been forthcoming. I am not here, as I have told your Lordship, in any way to snatch an advantage. I have treated this case with all the candour and openness which I think its importance demands. I have looked through all the despatches which have been open to me and I have tendered them in evidence. My learned friend looked through the despatches as he himself says. He kept my despatches out. Now, my lord, what is the inference to be drawn from that? What inference could common sense draw except that my learned friend is afraid of them?

Mr. Hannen—As to the period for which there are no records in English in the Consulate these remarks don't apply.

Mr. Havllar—There is not a word of evidence that the Chinese documents themselves are not there. My learned friend was at liberty to use my translations, I gave them to him, he cannot impugn their genuineness; there they are, they have been offered to the court, they have been kept out by my learned friend. I thought documents referring to a period over which memory cannot be expected to extend with any great accuracy—I thought ignorantly that they formed the best kind of evidence. My learned friend has taught me better.

His Lordship—Excuse me a moment, with reference to that matter. Mr. Hannen, I inferred from what you said yesterday that Mr. Playfair's search had been in reference to the Chinese documents as well.

Mr. Hannen—That was one particular thing which was suggested to me in the course of the trial.

His Lordship—Your observation applies to the Chinese documents?

Mr. Hannen—It does; Mr. Playfair searched.

Mr. Hayllar—But there are a great many other despatches which my learned friend has kept out, not only within that period but within recent periods. I would have been very glad, could I have done it, to have laid before your Lordship all the despatches, because I think the real truth of this case lies in the despatches. From the peculiar way in which affairs with reference to land are conducted, namely, through the authorities, surely the best evidence of what took place, if not the best evidence legally—I mean the best evidence as a matter of accuracy and genuineness, are the despatches. My learned friend has kept mine out, that is all that is to be said.

His Lordship—Is there no record kept in the Consulate here of leases in perpetuity?

Mr. Hayllar—Yes.

Mr. Sinclair—There is a register.

Mr. Hannen—Is not this agreement of 1867 registered?

Mr. Sinclair—Not in the land register.

Mr. Hannen—But it is put somewhere else?

Mr. Sinclair—It is in an iron chest.

Mr. Hayllar—There is no registration fee paid on it?

Mr. Sinclair—No.

His Lordship—What is this register?

Mr. Sinclair—They are registered in a book and numbered. There is the name of the lessor, the name of the lessee, and sometimes the terms. Agreements of rent are not registered.

Mr. Hannen—But this agreement has a number and is there in an envelope and a fee has been paid for whatever was done.

Mr. Sinclair—No fee has been paid.

Mr. Hannen—Not a fee of one dollar?

Mr. Sinclair—I think not.

Mr. Hannen—My client says he paid $1 for what he thought was the registration, and that the document was numbered.

Mr. Sinclair—The number is very likely its number among the documents deposited; every document deposited receives a number and is put into an iron chest.

His Lordship—I am asking Mr. Sinclair now—you say this document has not been registered?

Mr. Sinclair—No, not in the land register.

Mr. Hayllar—All I say about this is, that considering the knowledge of the Chinese on the subject, and the knowledge which I say was with Mr. Wolfe on the subject, the fact that the document was not recorded shows that it had no character of permanence about it and that that was a fact which was perfectly well understood by all the parties. My lord, I only use that as corroborative testimony, because I argue that, uncontradicted, your Lordship has no alternative standing as it does, but to accept the evidence of these high officers of the Government of China that I called before your Lordship as the correct exposition of the law. My learned friend pointed out one or two apparent discrepancies between the evidence of the old gentleman, the Prefect, who has been for so many years here, and the present Haukwan District Magistrate, who is at present administering the law in a very large district here, the discrepancy being as to whether a Chinese lease was made out in duplicate or not. I believe it is not, generally. I believe, the more correct opinion was expressed by the Haukwan District Magistrate. But that is a difference really not in the slightest degree affecting their credibility on a point of law which they were prepared to give evidence upon and which they had themselves deliberately looked up. If a lawyer, or doctor, or any body else, is taken into the witness box to give scientific evidence, it is a perfectly different thing from his being taken into the box to give evidence of a fact, because he would have prepared himself on the subject and looked up documents relating to it, and I have here sheaves of leases which have been looked up for me from all parts between Chinese themselves and between Chinese and foreigners, and I say the evidence of these gentlemen who are brought here, unless they are perjured men, is conclusive on the subject. And are they perjured men? Surely my learned friend could have brought something, some tittle, some jot of testimony from the various friends he has about him to contradict this evidence, if it could be contradicted, and yet it stands on your Lordship's notes absolutely uncontradicted. Now, who are these gentlemen? One of them has attained a very high rank indeed in the government service; he was brought down here from Peking about that wall business and abo it other business which I did not know might not form matters in dispute. He happened to have been the Prefect here during that critical period when all this went on about the negotiations for the wall and the lease of 1867. He was here at that time. I placed him in the box asking him such questions as were necessary for my case. My learned friend did not cross-examine him on these points. However, the matter did not become of much importance, because I used him chiefly as an expert, a man whose duty it is to adiminister the law, and who has had forty years' experience of it. Now it is not an abstruse point of law, it is not one on which there can be much difference of opinion. It is a common point, and I would ask your Lordship to enquire either from foreign officials or Chinese whether these persons are not the right persons for me to have placed in the box. Of course your Lordship has not been in China so long as to know all the little ins and outs of these things, nor do many foreigners know them, but the position of these two men is too high for them to come forward and risk it—it would be known everywhere that they had told one thing in this court and were administering another sort of law in their own courts if what they have stated was not correct. My learned friend's clients, who have not a very little position in the city, could have found all that out, but there the evidence stands on your Lordship's notes as the exposition of the law of China on the subject, and, as I shall show your Lordship, it jumps with the real meaning of the document and with what my learned friend has finally rested his case upon, namely, natural justice.

Now, my Lord, leaving for a moment, that subject of foreign law, I am anxious to meet my friend on that very ground of natural justice. He says, where there is no law—I have shown there is a law—where there is no law it is not English law that is to be applied, that being a thing which was brought out by your Lordship's pushing home rather an important question about English law; my learned friend to a certain extent, as it were, scouted English law, and then puts in an opinion that if it is not to be tried by Chinese law, then it must be tried according to the principles of natural justice.

I have laid before your Lordship the birth, growth, and coming to maturity of what is known in China as a missionary ri·t. I have shown your Lordship the steps by which they come to their full growth, and it is an illustration of the patient, curious character of the people among who n we are, who watch while you think they are not watching, who remember things which you think have passed out of their memory as not being of the slightest importance, but who pile up their injuries one upon another, it may be from father to son, at last to break out at some final piece of aggravation. Now, you see my lord, this port was only opened in the year 1843. Missionaries were not exactly in the contemplation of the Government of England or of the Government of China when this port was opened. In the second paragraph of the treaty of Nanking, which opened this port, the words are used "His Majesty the Emperor of China agrees that British subjects, with their families and establishments, shall be allowed to reside, for the purpose of carrying on their mercantile pursuits, without molestation or restraint, at the cities and towns of Canton, Amoy, Foochow-fu, Ningpo, and Shanghai." Now Foochow is a city of literates; the literary element is universally said by all standard books, which your Lordship may consult on the subject, to be very strong here, and for seven years after the opening of the port apparently there was very little trade and foreigners were very little known.

His Lordship—It is, I suppose, the Athens of China.

Mr. Hayllar—No, but it is a place full of literary people who have made it their home. It is a very old place. On the rocks at Wu-shih-shan there are inscriptions twelve hundred years old, in many languages, one being in Sanscrit. The city is a place with a very strong literary element in it, and before 1850, so far as I can discover, the people knew nothing of that particular product of civilisation, the Protestant missionary. Before 1850, a gentleman or two, Mr. Canting and Mr. Morrison, had been allowed to reside in this temple. The history of these things is this, when a new place is opened the foreigners' eclectic tastes are scarcely suited by ordinary Chinese buildings and there is nothing else for a foreigner to reside in except the temples. The temples are generally built in Chinese cities in the finest, the airiest, and the most beautiful positions. If your Lordship will go through any part of China you will see that to be the case. They are very desirable places, and the Chinese Go ernment, finding strangers without dwellings, kindly place these temples at their disposal, as they have recently done at Wenchow. Now here we had had before the missionaries came an admirable experience of a merchant and a Government official. The Government official was Mr. Morrison, who had come to live in one of our temples. He had treated us with the most perfect candour and fairness, he had not altered it except as we allowed him to do it, and he had gone away. But in 1850 there wander into the city two gentlemen whose calling, to the literates and to everybody else, is more or less of a mystery—they don't know much about them, but they know they are foreigners; foreigners have obtained a good name as quiet people, and they are placed in a temple in precisely the same way as previous foreigners. That these foreigners were the *avant couriers* of a string of other foreigners coming with like objects could never have entered into the minds of these literates. That their object could be otherwise than mercantile, or having a good deal of the mercantile element about it, could never be known to the authorities, because they had only given permission by treaty for people to come here for mercantile pursuits, and the idea of their Temple being used as it subsequently has been used for thirty years came as a complete revelation to them. How should they know anything about it? The priest of the temple, doubtless at the order—it does not matter whether it is at the order, let us say at the desire of the Chinese Government—gives these two foreigners Welton and Jackson, permission to dwell in two of their sacred buildings, one of which I believe is called the Five Fairies' Temple. They kindly, and with that exquisite courtesy which marks the Chinese mandarin when he desires to be friendly, remove the gods and give these people permission to use this place as a residence (your Lordship sees by the deed of 1850 there is nothing but residence mentioned) and it could not have entered anybody's mind that that was not all that was wanted. They give them permission to alter the inside of the premises to suit their convenience, a thing which they did not mind. Any alteration to the inside of the premises they were at liberty to make, and then they might reside there, possibly at their option. Well, these gentlemen did so, as far as I know, with the most complete good faith. Others came, perhaps not so wise in their generations, perhaps with university education, and so on, but not altogether trained fully in the ways of the world or Chinese philosophy or ideas. They perhaps did not know all about the way in which the original persons got possession of the temples, and they began, when they came, to treat them in a different way. Very well. We then find alterations beginning. Houses that were let to them are turned into a different kind of structures and so on, and as time goes on and the missionary interest in China grows a little bigger, it by and bye becomes a subject of treaty. Between this time and the year 1860 there is another war, and there is put into the treaty of 1860 an article known as Article 8, dealing specially with missionary subjects, upon which I have a word or two to say. Now this is a very remarkable article in its wording. The Chinese are always being told that these missionaries are men coming here with high and holy aims, they are always being told to put up proclamations of that kind, stating that they are come to do them good, although it must be admitted the upper classes don't like their doctrines (but that is neither here nor there) and they are told by this article itself what very excellent people these missionaries are. This says—"The Christian religion, as professed by Pr testants or R man Catholics, inculcates the practice of virtue, and teaches man to do as he would be done by."

His Lordship—It only speaks of the doctrine.

Mr. Hayllar—But the Chinese would naturally suppose the people inculcating that doctrine would be the persons who would deal fairly with them. But after that maxim put in in that way comes another, like a beautiful insect with a tremendous sting in its tail. "Persons teaching it or professing it," says this article, "shall be entitled to the protection of the Chinese authorities," which is all very well—"nor shall any such, peaceably pursuing their calling and n t offending against the laws be persecuted or interfered wit ." Now, my lord, had your Lordship been here long enough to have become acquainted with what has been done under that article of the treaty, your Lord hip might have been prepared to project your mind with some fresh light in it upon the meaning of what my learned friend calls in his answer our "acquiescence." Acquiescence has a good many meanings. Your Lordship does not suppose this was an article very acceptable, nor was it one very easy to construe, but the literature contained in the hundreds of blue books with reference to missionary questions in China, if it shows anything, shows that up to 1871, when the question was finally decided against their pretensions, missionaries did assume to themselves under that article much more than the privileges of the mere *Civis Romanus*. They became very awkward customers to deal with indeed, and that was the kind of reputation which they liked to get. It was a useful one. In the rear was the force of the British Empire, her armies, her fleets, and her gunboats so often called in to repress disturbance or difficulty. In the front was the missionary with his treaty, with his splendid precept at the beginning, and his right not to be interfered with at the end. That was the position. Now, my lord, after a war which had resulted in this treaty with this kind of thing in it, it is not to be wondered at that the authorities became extremely timid. The missionaries were emboldened in proportion as the authorities were intimidated—I am upon the question now of natural justice—the gentry and the authorities saw these things going on. My learned friend says they were probably very much incensed. They were, indeed, very much incensed. They were piling their injuries up in their minds, not forgetting them, and they sometimes even ventured to remonstrate. But such remonstrances were bound to be snubbed, not by Mr. Sinclair, decidedly, for I must say the copies of the dispatches laid before me show an equitable fairness of dealing in all these matters in that quarter. The people hesitated to come forward. How were they to understand how to prevent the things they objected to, how to assert their rights? They have a way in the background, at first by offering other terms, and unfortunately when that fails they, knowing no better, resort to violence. The Chinese mind and the Chinese temper will bear a great deal before it is forced into active hostility against any foreigner, much less a missionary, and therefore they doubtless did stand by and see many things done to which they objected. But what is to be said of those who did them? There they are, placed temporarily, as they well know, on land which if there is any certainty about the law of China, is most certainly inalienable, which has never been let in the history of the world, as far as we know, except to foreigners, and then only because other sites could not be obtained. They find themselves in a position which they like and which, if they can, they intend to stick to. Naturally too, for it is a beautiful site. It was chosen as such, as the sites of all temples are. Therefore, forsooth this temple here and all the rights of this great city, are to be sacrificed to the demands of these missionaries, utterly unfounded in common sense, law, or justice, because they ask for it. My lord, if they had contented themselves simply with asking for it it would not have mattered so much, but bearing about him the charmed life of a foreigner, a person not subject to the strict discipline of the bamboo, the foreigner does what would bring a Chinaman to instant grief. He begins to tamper with the guardian of the temple, the old man that he has about him, whom he sees in his daily life, and whom he by cajolery and bribes induces to make documents utterly false and wholly nefarious. That is how the truth of the matter stands. That is the natural justice of this business. Not caring what becomes of the old man, utterly regardless of the broken career of this poor old heathen, although he had before him the fact that making a deed with this old man about another matter had brought him to punishment—no matter whether it was the Blind Man's Temple or what it was—the foreigner again brings the old man into the power of the authorities and leads him into a danger which is simply the brink of the grave for him.

My Lord, I cross-examined Mr. Wolfe, to whom I am alluding, in these remarks—I cross-examined him with a severity which my learned friend has termed bullying. I don't regret one of the questions I put to Mr. Wolfe, nor do I regret the severity which the cross-examination assumed, and I shall, I think—and this is of importance at this part of the case as showing something else—I think I shall show your Lordship that on two or three points Mr. Wolfe's evidence is palpably untrue, and through the whole of it completely shifty. *Non mi recordo*—I don't remember, was the burden of his evidence. My Lord, at the end of my learned friend's examination of his own witness, in order to contradict some paragraph in my petition, my learned friend, who of course was acting on instructions, asked a question about certain negotiations which had taken place in 1878, which I had alleged in my petition as having taken place, perhaps a trifle too briefly. However, as we shall see, they are substantially true. Mr. Wolfe, in answer to his own counsel, says, "I know nothing of any negotiations having taken place with the high authorities in England." My learned friend is so completely left in ignorance by his client that he asked me if by the "high authorities" I meant the Missionary Society, which I certainly did not. Mr. Wolfe goes on, "having taken place in 1878 as stated in the 24th paragraph of the petition. If any such negotiations did take place I had nothing to do with them. If by the high authorities in England is meant the Church Missionary Society they had nothing to do with it." I am sorry to say that is not quite true. Now, my lord, yesterday Mr. Stewart is put in the box and he produces a letter which leads to my asking in re-examination a few pertinent questions of Mr. Sinclair And then it turns out that the negotiations which Mr. Wolfe had told me in cross-examination, varying from his statement in his examination-in-chief, only had reference to a building he was going to place on a piece of land bought from King Po—in truth had reference to an offer made by Ting Futai to purchase the whole of this piece of property—and that the business had gone so far that Mr. Sinclair had actually written home to the Foreign Office on the subject and had referred to it in a letter to Mr. Stewart as a reason for stating that he should have preferred not giving any permission to build until an answer to his letter had come. Now, my lord, that negotiation had been communicated personally by Mr. Sinclair to Mr. Wolfe, and I ask what is the meaning of that evidence? Was it not obvious to any mind, dealing with my petition, knowing the subject, that that negotiation was what I referred to. So there we begin at one of the few points at which we have an opportunity of testing Mr. Wolfe's accuracy by independent testimony. We find there at least a very considerable inaccuracy. That, I say, characterises his evidence throughout. And then there comes a transaction or two which I have already referred to, and which I don't intend to go through at any length. Mr. Wolfe says he tried to get the Blind Man's Temple, and in proof of that he produces a minute from his minute books with reference to the purchase of this temple. I with great candour admitted that as evidence. I noticed, however, there was no minute produced with reference to the $500 deed. I don't know whether there is such a minute or whether there is not. At any rate, it is not here, yet there is one with reference to the purchase of the Blind Man's Temple. Well, all I can say about that is that it only adds one more grievance to those I know of. I did not know before I came into this court that any effort had been made to buy the Blind Man's Temple alone, but your Lordship sees there is a curious sort of admission in that minute that it is known that if this thing were attempted to be carried through there would be some difficulty, because they use the words "if it prove successful," clearly showing there was in the minds of the Finance Committee a doubt whether they could buy this temple. Now, Mr. Wolfe says this was the transaction which led to the imprisonment of the priest. But the funny part of it is that Mr. Wolfe is thereby placed in such a dilemma that he is unable to say either one way or the other whether that document was ever reduced to writing, whether, in point of fact, the transaction about the $400 for the temple ever took the form of an agreement. Well, if it did not, how could we know anything about it, how could the authorities have known anything about it and imprisoned the priest? If it did, why is there no reference to the document in the despatches with reference to the release of Chun Yuen Ching; why, in point of fact, is a totally different document referred to? I don't believe myself that it ever took the form of a document, because our archives are so carefully kept and we have no record of it, but the fact that he tried to buy the Blind Man's Temple is not questioned, for the earth hunger at this particular period of his career was very strong on Mr. Wolfe, as we shall see, and it might well be that when he began to talk and tamper, as I put it, with the old priest, the Blind Man's Temple as well as a great deal more came under consideration. The "tumultuous orgies" in the temple were most likely as offensive to the gentleman who was favouring us with his society in the temple, where we don't want him, as his presence was to us. Not only was he anxious to get rid of the "tumultuous orgies" of these poor blind men whom he wished to deprive of their place of recreation, but he probably said to himself, "Surely if we can get rid of the blind men we can get rid of a great many who are not blind, we can get rid of the people coming into our ground by making a very clean sweep by purchasing not only the property we have now, but a great deal which lies outside the walls." My lord, in support of that view of the man's evidence I produce the deed for $800. All my learned friend can say about that deed is that it perhaps was the work of some zealous subordinate. Well, there may be zealous subordinates, but any zealous subordinate who forged that document must have had a curious insight into my mind, because it was only I myself who selected the documents for my petition. I have had them a long time, and that these documents had any bearing upon the case is due to my perhaps—as my learned friend would say—misplaced ingenuity. That a cancelled document should be forged and put away is a novelty in the history of forgeries, unless by people so diabolically ingenious that they can read the future. It was simply put in my petition because it happened to be the first of the series which I found, and the $400 deed, if it ever existed, would have answered my purpose just as well—indeed perhaps better. But the $800 deed does not answer Mr. Wolfe's purpose, and I will show your Lordship how it does not answer his purpose directly. It does not answer his purpose because your Lordship sees he says he paid $500 down when he made the second deed, and having admitted he had not paid any dollars down with reference to the $400 transaction he had to give some reason for it. Now the reason for not paying the $400 was because he thought he might fail in the purchase of the temple, but he did not think it was in the least degree likely he would fail in purchasing the whole of the property. Oh! no, there was no doubt about that—he had no reason to doubt it! So the witness hums and haws a great deal about this document, whether he had seen it or had not, and about his teacher, but at last he pledges himself, I think, to the fact that he ne er did see it. He thus, as he thinks, gets rid of a perfectly unanswerable argument, that if he had failed in that he certainly would not have paid the $500 on the other. Now that is where the priest's story is so likely. I must say, in drawing any comparison between these two ministers of different religions as to straightforwardness and telling even things damaging to himself, the palm lies with the Buddhist, and the truth lies with him. Now, the $500 deed being made—I am not going to draw your Lordship's attention to it much more except to make one very significant observation. I told you Mr. Wolfe had something in his mind which prevented his acknowledging the truth about the Priest being imprisoned for the $500 deed, and it was this, if he had paid $500 to the priest and he had not got the property, would Mr. Carroll have alluded to the priest as an innocent man? Would he not after that transaction rather have alluded to him as an old vagabond?

Mr. Hannen—My learned friend complained of my having kept out documents. He has been for the last half-hour commenting on a document which is not in.

Mr. Hayllar—But I contend it is in. My learned friend produced a witness, Mr. Sinclair, and laid that before him. I cross-examined upon it and therefore I have a right to allude to it. And there is the fact that the man is alluded to as an innocent man, and I put it he would not have been alluded to as an innocent man if he had had the $500. Of course with regard to the promissory note, if the $500 had been previously paid on the deed the transaction takes a slightly modified form; it is not quite so bad as it is if the priest has told the truth. But looking at the document itself, did any body ever read in the history of usury such an extraordinary thing as the converting of a lease into what is tantamount to an absolute assignment by a three years' purchase? Whoever heard in the history of equity of such a transaction as that, and yet, my Lord, that is done in the teeth of a treaty—and we are upon natural justice—which says, it is article 12, "British subjects whether at t e ports or ther p aces, desiring to build or open h uses, wareh uses, churches, hospitals, or burial grounds, shall make t eir agreement for the land or buildings they require, at the rates prevailing among the people, equitably, and without exaction on either side." At the rates prevailing among the people for the finest site in the city of Foochow! obviously so to anybody who goes there—$500 and something like 26 per cent. interest a year! Now, I ask your Lordship if that is not where the natural justice which my learned friend relies on comes in? The natural justice is with us.

Now, after the shaking which Mr. Wolfe had got about the former deed, one certainly is a little surprised at the pertinacity of the man. The priest absconds and his absconding may have been a fact which was a benefit to Mr. Wolfe or not—I don't know, perhaps not, perhaps it would have been better for him if the priest had stayed, because if the priest had stayed the transaction could have been hushed up probably, or possibly, for three or four years, and then the document might have been sprung upon us, and as no rent had been paid the property would have been the missionaries'. But the priest had to run away to avoid his just deserts brought upon him, be it remembered, by a person who was bound by treaty to inculcate the practice of virtue upon him; yet I do not suppose his ruin had been intentionally brought about, as Mr. Wolfe probably would have preferred it the other way, but as things turned out this document became a rather ticklish business. On this subject my accusation against Mr. Wolfe is that he did not pay the rent till he was ordered to do so. That is very plain to my mind, as I read the evidence in the case. But he does not say so—I don't know exactly what he does say in fact—all he admits is that he met some directors in his garden and they had a conversation, the substance of which is not very clear, but the effect is, that is how the fact came out that the rent was not paid, and a complaint was made, and then he asks the opinion of his Consul, as he says, whether it was reasonable he should pay the rent or not. That is the most extraordinary thing I ever heard of, obviously his intention still being in 1867 to hang on to his rights under the promissory note if he could make use of it.

Then comes the transaction in which a little of the natural justice I think is again on our side. Instead of telling him then, as we might have done "really these things are of such a kind that we cannot trust you in the least degree," by the friendly intercession of the Consul another document is drawn up—these patient long-suffering people, who don't want the rent, but simply desire to give these gentlemen the facilities for carrying on their work, draw up a document against which Mr. Wolfe cannot prevent himself from making a nasty imputation, to the effect that nobody called it to his notice that the words about the option of continuing to hire the premises were left out. Now, whose business was it to call it to his notice? Here is a gentleman who had been then five years in the country. I just led him on a little about his knowledge of Chinese, about the deed of 1866, to test a little his knowledge of Chinese, because by that time I had some experience of Mr. Wolfe's method of giving evidence, and then it became clear that he had advanced so far as to be able to read the agreement with his teacher (and he admitted that he generally did read his documents), and having done so he wrote "I agree to the above terms," having the terms before him. Now, where is the want of natural justice or equity on our part there? Surely by this time we had had enough experience of these gentlemen to reserve to ourselves the power of getting rid of them at such time as they carried their practices past all endurance. Now that is exactly what we find they have done. We find them building a cross wall, to which I cannot discover what title they have at all. In 1866 they were working under what Mr. Wolfe under his own signature admits were false deeds. The answer these persons would give no doubt is, this wretched Chinese Government won't have foreigners buying land in the City. We won't have them buying land around that temple, but they may build in any convenient place they can find. Have we not offered them other places? But we look at these transactions from a totally different stand point. We say that they are surreptitious and offensive in the last degree to our laws. They get hold of some chair-bearer, some Taouist priest, some fellow or other who will sell anything, and then try by such means, to get possession of land and by not registering their deeds to secure their ends. These practices were still going on, until after 1867 it was found it would not do to carry them on, and so things went on for some time quietly. Well, then comes 1871. There is a bungalow up to the end of 1870 where that elevated structure (pointing to the model) now stands. That was burned down and this building was substituted for it. Mr. Wolfe himself admitted that if he had been here he would not have built that building; he knew it was offensive to our prejudices. But I put it not only on that ground; not only was it offensive to our prejudices, it was also a source of danger. So he goes on up to 1876. Then he is again at the same work; he pulls down that wall, he buys a piece of land from a Buddhist priest that turns out to be public land, and he builds another wall. After a deal of trouble the wall is ordered to be pulled down by the Consul; it is rebuilt again and there it stands. Well, then he turns that building, without any permission whatever, the understanding being that they should only be residences —he turns that building into a girls' school, just close to the temple, of all places in the world to put a girls' school. He then obtains permission from Mr. Sinclair—Mr. Sinclair not being aware of the details of the question whether that piece of land on which he put the ruined house came in under the lease of 1867 or not; Mr. Sinclair was not here in the time of Mr. Smith, as far as I know, and it is not for him to know a piece of land let verbally—Mr. Wolfe obtains permission to put that building on a piece of ground which he says now is included in the lease of 1867. We say it is not, and the only evidence for the defendant on the subject, as a matter of natural justice, appears to have been Mr. Wolfe's imagination. I asked him if he made any inquiry; he said, no. Of course he didn't make any inquiry, because if he had he would have known what it would have led to. There is the want of natural justice in not making inquiries which would lead to awkward revelations. He makes no inquiry, he commences the building, I say throwing dust in the eyes of Mr. Sinclair.

The piece of land let by the priest was the piece he pointed out; the man was the witness of truth throughout, and it stands to reason that was the piece, because if it had not been a piece marked out by its own natu al boundaries some better identification of it would have been given, but being as it is a sort of *bellevedere* its own boundaries are marked out, whereas on the other piece there are no natural limits and it would have been described by metes and bounds. It would have been described with still greater certainty if it had been land let for building purposes. Well, our evidence being entirely uncontradicted, they commence this building, and then Mr. Stewart, who has just come, as he tells us, with the polish of Trinity College, Dublin, upon him, a very desirable addition to the place, no doubt—he comes here and he has the charge of these transactions. Mr. Stewart was burning with anxiety to be cross-examined yesterday, he was placed in the box to be cr ss-examined, but his evidence as it stood was so exceedingly favourable to the view I take of the transaction that I thought it wiser to leave so formidable an antagonist alone; so he has given his evidence with the honour of not being cross-examined. However, we take it from him that he got the permission from Mr. Sinclair in a very carefully worded letter to build only until there came some opposition from the gentry; and, said my learned friend to him, "Did any opposition come?" "Yes, I received a request from Mr. Sinclair to discontinue building," "And you declined?" Well, there Mr. Stewart lengthened out into a history of how he came to decline by referring to documents with extreme volubility, and your Lordship said it would be better that he should answer the question, and he accordingly did so, and he said he did decline. So Mr. Stewart comes into the box to represent himself as a gentleman who, in a very important matter, has broken a solemn promise. That is the attitude in which the second missionary of this society stands before your Lordship. Having obtained from the Consul this permission, he pooh-poohs that authority, and the opinion of that kindly gentleman, who has so great a knowledge of the Chinese, who has lived among them the better part of his life, who knows the signs of a gathering storm and that in these countries things are not perhaps quite so fair as they seem, and who knows perfectly well it is not a danger to be lightly risked. This gentleman of 1876, who has been here two years, from Trinity College, Dublin, knows all about fung shui and the views of these people! and he says "I am not going to stop my works, I am only doing them inside." Well, but was not Mr. Sinclair perfectly right? Whether he was doing them inside or out the feeling might have been allayed if the Chinese had seen that Mr. Stewart had shown the slightest signs of keeping good faith, that he was not going on putting in doors and windows and making this property, which had to be pulled down, as everyone knew, more valuable, and which the Chinese knew from former experience they would have to pay very stiffly for—that is always the end of these cases, the Chinese have to pay—and so they go on. Well, the storm did break and the Chinese destroyed a piece of building which was theirs, which they had a perfect right to deal with as they liked, only they took the unfortunate form of doing it by violence. That I don't stand here to justify; it is a pity, but it is what every one must have known would have happened.

Now, one further word as to natural justice, that pure equity to which my learned friend appeals. A very distinguished governor of this place indeed, Ting, a man whose name is known throughout China as one of the most distinguished men in it, seeing the position of affairs, knowing the dangers that were rising, knowing how suddenly a storm breaks, how difficult it is to quell, and how much China has always to pay—because the attitude of complete firmness which these missionary gentlemen take up always leads in the end to something better for them—seeing all these things Ting did, through Mr. Sinclair, make an offer, the liberality of which is I think unquestioned. That telegraph place, which they turn up their noses at, cost the Government, as I have found by inquiry, $17,000, and they could have let it, and still can let it at any moment, for $1,000 a year. We have only been holding it over for their benefit. This they might have had as a free gift with another piece of land and $5 0 besides, and it is while this magnificent offer, dealing with the natural justice of the question, is standing before them that Mr. Stewart goes on with his work. Now I don't think, with this little tale to meet, my learned friend has any right to appeal to natural justice. I say it is the pushing of a dominant race, with energy and with all the power behind it of a mighty empire, against an old, good natured, and apathetic one. That is the true pith of this case. If it had been legitimate pushing, if the pushing had not taken the form as I say it did of aggression and tricks, it would not have so much mattered, but that that is the form it did take no one who has heard the evidence in this court can in the slightest degree doubt.

Now, my lord, these are the two points on which I say the case has been placed. My learned friend, by putting in that document which he did, or rather by laying the law before you, by his own admission removes the case, or he wishes to remove the case, from the domain of strict English law, and he appeals to your Lordship to deal with the matter equitably. I think the case clearly stands on foreign law, but if it is to go on the second ground your Lordship must look at the transactions from beginning to end.

But whether it goes on foreign law, as I contend it ought to go, or on natural justice, there are still one or two elements in the case which I have to call your Lordship's attention to in the briefest possible manner which I think even natural justice must take notice of. And the first is, what is the position which this society takes up? I don't understand it myself. It is a fluctuating body of subscribers, here to-day and there to-morrow; you don't know who is the body or how it is be affected by any decree. Should Mr. Wolfe leave this place who are we to look to for our rent? Who is to be his successor? My learned friend speaks of Mr. Wolfe's predecessors. That is the mischief of the thing. We might like one gentleman with whom we made an agreement for rent, as we might have liked Messrs. Welton and Jackson; we don't like another, as may be, for sake of example, Mr. Stewart. And is Mr. Stewart to have the benefit of Mr. Wolfe's contract, or who is to have it? The ideas, doubtless, of the Government of China, or whoever does these things, the directors of the temple, are greatly modified, like those of all Chinese and indeed of people all over the world, by personal considerations. They have, for instance, the greatest faith in the fair dealing with their property of the English Government. The English Consul has as a summer residence a small temple, as your Lordship must have seen personally on your visit to Wu Shih Shau. The English Government, through its officers here, has preserved towards the Chinese Government in dealing with that temple that kind of faith which your Lordship knows is called *uberrima fides*. Mr. Welton and Mr. Jackson may have d ne the same for all I know. We say Mr. Wolfe has not. We gave him a document which was meant to be an annual lease, and we say "As you have not preserved that kind of faith with us we don't make a contract with anybody to follow you." Mr. Stewart—I don't know whether he is to be here or whether he is not—Mr. Stewart is unfortunately the gentleman who has broken his promise to the Consul. That is known perfectly well to the Chinese; therefore they don't believe in him, and it would be a very hard thing on the directors of this temple if any decree of this court could leave it in the hands of Mr. Wolfe or anybody else to select a successor. We should like to select him ourselves. But that is not all; the law steps in, and why a missionary society, because it is a missionary society, or for any reason on earth, say because it is in China, should have a different status from what it has in any other part of the world, merely because it is a society established in England for certain high purposes—I don't know why, I say, such a society should have any privilege higher than if I associated myself with other people for any purpose in the world. Therefore it stands that the true reading of the document of 1867 is as a personal contract with Mr. Wolfe. When we came to give a more formal document (we certainly did it in one particular in a very clumsy manner, because we gave it to Mr. Wolfe and others; the document itself is made with others, but those others are not named) the intention is made obvious that the tenancy should continue after Mr. Wolfe went away. The passing out of the port of any missionary, as far as the Chinese are concerned, is equivalent to his passing into a better world—they know no more of him, and therefore the idea of the document itself is clear, and it goes to show what was the intention of the document of 1867, that it should be personally, with Mr. Wolfe. But what the missionaries wanted all along, as shown by their promissory note, and what they want now is that they should get a decree that the property should be made over to their society, a thing impossible, because there is nothing it could be made over to. My learned friend did not touch upon that in his speech, although I asked Mr. Wolfe about it in the first instance and put it in the forefront of my case.

My learned friend also has not contradicted my evidence about these Chinese associations. In point of fact, so far from contradicting it he acknowledged through Mr. Wolfe the existence of one of these societies, namely, the Blind Man's Association. Now could a decree be made to cover associations of this kind? No. And the real meaning of it is that it never was meant to do so, it was not meant to be a formal document of that kind, either on the part of the Missionary Society or the Associations, for the simple reason that the thing was impossible. The property never having been let in the history of time before foreigners came here it was not in the contemplation of anybody to from a kind of association for the letting of the property. The directors were put in the document of 1867, not to give a higher or better title, not because they wanted to continue the tenancy, but in order to prevent the continuation of a fraud, and they were therefore, as I put it in my opening address, the mere channels through which the rent poured into the incense and lamp department of the temple. So much for the directors.

But before I sit down, there is one other point upon which also my learned friend offered no argument, to which I must refer. Whether we deal with the case by English law or natural justice we look for precedents in some way to guide us. Now, I have made a search so far as my limited powers of search could be extended in this place, and, indeed, before I came here, to find if there was referred to in any book any English document anything like this form, with such words as "May not be let to anybody else" in it. I have found nothing of the kind in English law; the words in fact are utterly unknown. They are in a foreign language. These are the words around which the battle rages. But the "may not be let to any one else" is an expression unknown only in English drafting; therefore if we have to deal with it on the basis of natural justice we know perfectly well what it means in China. We may also look to see what the words actually do mean. My learned friend wants to import, as I understand his contention, another word which we have in our language, which we know perfectly well, and which occurs in the same document in another sentence; he wants to import the word "resume." To make his contention according to natural justice—and I am anxious to turn this case in every light before your Lordship's eyes—my learned friend wants to import into his reading of that expression the word "resume." The word "resume" being there, accompanying these same words in another part of the document "may resume and/or let to any one else" clearly shows that according to the natural meaning of the words in the same document there is a distinction between the two. We have a term which we translate "resume," but which literally means "take back." The words are there and are "may resume and/or let to any one else." Therefore, according to that kind of reading of the case which my learned friend wants, I think he is entirely out of court; I think it would not be competent for the court to add a term to this contract which is not there, which is certainly known to the writers of it, and which occurs in the same document in another place. Looking at it in that light, without any reference to its being a common term among the Chinese, simply on the basis which my learned friend puts it on, I think your Lordship could only make a decree that "they should not let it to any one else." Your Lordship has on your notes the cases in English law on the subject and I don't intend to touch upon them any more. The case I handed up to your Lordship last night is only a case which is referred to in other cases about an agreement not to give a notice to quit being repugnant to an annual lease. That is what I quoted as the decision of an Irish court. Therefore I say on English law pure and simple the law is with us, and on natural justice and on English and foreign law I ask your Lordship for a declaration of our rights. What form the decree would take would depend. I apprehend, supposing your Lordship is in our favour, on which of these branches your Lordship decides it upon. The form the decree would take if it were for the defendants would naturally be very simple, but the form a decree for the plaintiffs would take would depend upon one of three points. If your Lordship accepted, as I contend you are bound to do, Chinese law, then I apprehend the non-acceptance of rent for nine months, would according to their books, be the foundation for an order or decree that the lease had ceased. I presume that if that were the case my learned friend, of course subject to his appealing, would not go any further. I did not bring the case in the form of an action simply for ejectment, because I had some doubt in my mind as to which law your Lordship would think would prevail. If it is English law of course they would have to the end of the year if your Lordship could find a date. According to English law their notice would have to expire at the end of a year. That has not yet expired; the suit did not take that form. But if your Lordship is of opinion that the lease has expired according to Chinese custom the form of your decree I suppose will say so, and if your Lordship gives that decree we shall know how to deal with it. I presume the matter would end there.

Now, my Lord, I leave the case in your hands to do equity in any way your Lordship shall think right. We are not dealing with this case as we do with a bill of exchange; it is a case for a declaration of rights and is not a case, of course, in which we desire to inflict hardship. Supposing your Lordship were to hold in our favour, I think any suggestion, or leaving it to ourselves to deal with it equitably, I may give my own word for it, would have the greatest weight. Supposing the decree to be in our favour, any terms we would offer are not things I can mention, but any suggestion from your Lordship would have great weight, at any rate with me, and I stand here in a responsible position in saying a thing of that kind.

His Lordship—Mr. Hayllar, with reference to the agreement of 1866 how can I give you any relief?

Mr. Hayllar—I don't ask for any. Your Lordship sees how the thing occurred. I made the gentry parties to begin with to represent this piece of property, as well as others, and they were struck out.

His Lordship—It was by a slip this paragraph was kept in, then?

Mr. Hayllar—It was not exactly by a slip, but there it is.

His Lordship—Then I understand you to say, with reference to the first prayer—

Mr. Hayllar—It may be struck out.

His Lordship—Then upon another point, paragraph 20, about that right of way?

Mr. Hayllar—I don't offer any evidence upon it, except that Mr. Wolfe himself said there was a path going across there and in point of fact there was.

His Lordship—Having regard to the importance of the case, I shall defer my judgment, and perhaps it may be as well I should state the course I intend to pursue with reference to that. What I propose to do is to send my judgment to Mr. Sinclair and ask him to be good enough to read it to the parties here.

The Court then rose.

JUDGMENT.

(Read at Foochow, July 19th.)

The following is the judgment of His Lordship in this case:—

The petition in this case, in its re-amended form, was filed on behalf of four of the directors of the Tao Shan Kwan Temple, situate at Wu Shih Shan in the city of Foochow, in the Empire of China, against the Reverend John Richard Wolfe, a British subject, and a clerk in Holy Orders, residing at Foochow, who was also sued on behalf of the English Church Missionary Society; and it prayed (1) that the rights of the parties interested in and under a certain lease of September, 1866, might be ascertained and declared; (2) that an agreement of rent dated August, 1867, between the defendant and Chow Taou Wen and Lin Yuen Chin, both now deceased, might be declared and decreed to be void; (3) that it might be ordered and decreed that the defendant had by his unauthorized and wrongful dealings with the land and buildings comprised in the agreement of August, 1867, forfeited all his right and title in and to such lands and buildings; (4) that the rights of the parties interested in that agreement might be ascertained and prescribed; (5) that the boundaries of the land comprised in the same agreement might be ascertained and declared; and (6) that the plaintiffs might have such further and other relief as the nature of the case might require. When the petition was amended the names of some of the original plaintiffs who alone claimed to be entitled to sue in respect of the agreement of September, 1866, were struck out; but the statement of that agreement, and the part of the prayer which related to it were retained in the petition. It did not therefore appear in the form in which the petition was presented to the court at the hearing of the cause what was the nature of the plaintiffs' interest in respect of the property comprised in the agreement of September, 1866, or how they were entitled to sue in respect of such agreement; and, in reply to a question touching such interest and right of suit addressed by the Court to Mr. Hayllar at the conclusion of his reply, that learned counsel said that he did not ask for any declaration by the Court in regard to that agreement. The questions, then, which the Court has to consider and determine are those which arise under and in connection with the agreement of August, 1867. The petition stated that the Tao Shan Kwan Temple, with the buildings and lands belonging thereto, was the property of the city of Foochow, that the direction and management of the temple lands and the control and expenditure of the funds belonging thereto were vested in directors duly appointed; that the plaintiffs, Chow Chang Kung, Lin King Chang, Loo King Fah and Sat Keok Min, were four of such directors and sued for themselves and the other directors; that by an agreement of rent dated the 18th December, 1850, Welton and Jackson, who were then the representatives at Foochow of the English Church Missionary Society, rented from a Taouist priest named Lin Yung Mow two houses situated respectively at the back and front of the left hand of the Tao Shau Kwan, which were described as follows:—One house with five rooms in a row, broadwise to which was attached an outhouse and an open yard at back and front. One house with four rooms in a row, broadwise at the back to which was attached an outhouse having an upper storey of two rooms and a lower storey of one room and an open yard. It was also thereby agreed that the rent of the above houses should be $100 per annum, and that rent for three months should be paid in advance according to the English Calendar; that the said Taouist priest should not interfere with or obstruct any works that might be going on or repairs that might be made inside the houses, which were to be done at the expense of the lessees; that it should be at the option of the lessees to continue the hiring of the said houses, and that the said Taouist priest should not be at liberty to let them to other persons. The document bore the Seal of the British Consulate and that of the Hau Kwan District Magistrate. The above two houses were of Chinese structure and were erected on land belonging to the Tao Shan Kwan Temple and formed part of the out-buildings of that Temple. It appeared in evidence that those houses were, subsequently to the date of the agreement of December, 1850, viz., the one in 1855, and the other in 1857 removed by the missionaries, and that in the place of one of them a large bungalow, which was used as a mission house, and in that of the other a residence, but which was now and had been since 1877 a girls' school, was built. Thus the character of the structures leased in 1850 was entirely altered. In 1855, Fearnley and Welton, who then represented the English Church Missionary Society at Foochow, entered into an agreement in the Chinese language with a Taouist priest of the Tao Shan Kwan Temple, named Chun Yuen Ching, whereby the Taouist priest agreed to let to Fearnley and Welton a row of four rooms going straight in, situated on the right hand side of the Tao Shan Kwan Temple, at an annual rent of $20 payable quarterly. It was also agreed that no rent should be allowed to fall into arrear, and that should it fall into arrear Chun Yuen Ching might resume and let the property to other persons, and that if rent was properly paid the property might not be let to anyone else. That document was not recorded at the British Consulate, nor did it bear either that seal or the seal of the Hau Kwan District Magistrate. The four rooms comprised in the last mentioned agreement consisted of three dwelling rooms and one servant's room. In or about the summer of 1863, the missionaries added an upper storey to those rooms. In 1861, one George Smith, deceased, who was a Missionary of the English Church Missionary Society, rented verbally a small piece of land contiguous to the temple for 12 dollars a year. One of the contests in the case was the site of this piece of land; the plaintiffs contending that it was on a hillock just outside the Tao Shau Kwan Temple, and the defendant that it lay to the North of the rooms let to Fearnley and Welton in 1855. Early in 1866 the defendant entered into a treaty with a priest of the Tao Shau Kwan Temple for the absolute purchase for the sum of 400 dollars of the Blind Man's Temple, which was a temple outside the Tao Shau Kwan Temple, and only a few yards from it; but the negotiation failed, the Tao Shan Kwan authorities having interfered to prevent the sale to Wolfe. About three or four months after the failure of that negotiation, Wolfe entered into another negotiation with the same priest for the absolute purchase for 1,500 dollars of the property then in his occupation and comprised in the agreements of 1850 and 1855, and in the verbal agreement to which the missionary George Smith was a party, and for all which premises he paid an aggregate annual rent of $132. But this negotiation likewise failed. There was no doubt, upon the evidence, that the priest at the Tao Shau Kwan had got into trouble with the authorities of the Temple through his negotiations for the sale to Wolfe of some of the Tao Shan Kwan property; and that such trouble was the cause of the agreement of August, 1867. Indeed, Wolfe himself in his evidence said, "I think the deed of 1867 arose out of my trouble with he priest." Wolfe's evidence in that respect confirmed what had been previously stated in his evidence by Loo King Fah, one of the plaintiffs, who said that "when it was found that there had been some strange or peculiar dealings between the Taouist priest and the missionaries, the Directors thought that they would themselves make a new agreement of rent with the missionaries." The same witness, Loo King Fah, said that one of the documents from which the agreement of August, 1867, was drawn, was the agreement of 1850, and that the directors of the temple who themselves framed the draft of the agreement of August, 1867, struck out the words "at the option of the lessees," which were in the agreement of 1850. The following is a translation of the agreement of August, 1867, which was in the Chinese language: "Agreement of rent. The British missionary John R. Wolfe agrees with the directors of the Tao Shau Kwan Temple to rent from them the following property, which was formerly, in the 30th year Tau Kwan, rented by the missionaries Welton and Jackson, namely, two houses situated respectively at the back and at the front of the left hand side of the Tao Shau Kwan [these two houses are as follow] 1. One five-roomed house with an outhouse and some waste ground at back and front. 2. One four-roomed house at the back with an outhouse having an upper storey and a lower storey of one room and a piece of waste ground. The rent of the above to be as of old, $100 per annum. Also (Mr. Wolfe agrees) to rent the following property which was originally rented in the fifth year Hsien Feng to the missionaries Welton and Fearnley, namely, four rooms on the right hand side of the Tao Shau Kwan, going straight in. The rent to be as of old, $20 per annum. Also, a small piece of land formerly hired under a verbal agreement by the missionary George Smith: the rent to be as of old, $ 2 per annum. These amount in all to a yearly sum of $132. The first instalment of which for the summer quarter, viz., $33, to be paid at once to the Trade Committee for transmission through the directors of the Temple to the Taouist priests, to be used in the service of the Temple. It is agreed that the same sum be paid quarterly in advance according to the English calendar to the Trade Committee for transmission, and the rent be not allowed to get into arrears. Should this happen, the directors may resume [or*] let the place to some one else. On the other hand if the rent does not get into arrears the place may not be let to any one else. Both parties being of the same mind, neither of them can withdraw. It is therefore considered advisable to draw up this agreement in triplicate, to be kept by the different parties.

Guarantor, CONSUL SINCLAIR.

Dated, August, 1867.

(Signed) CHOU TAOU WEN, LIN YUNE CHIN, } Directors of the Tao Shau Kwan.

I agree to the terms specified in the above agreement.

(Signed) JOHN R. WOLFE.

[Seal of Hau-kwan Magistrate.] [British Consular Seal.]

The two directors of the Tao Shau Kwan Temple who signed the above agreement are now dead. It will have been seen that the description of the houses mentioned in the agreement of August, 1867, was substantially the same as the descriptions of the houses mentioned in the agreements of 1850 and 1855; but in August, 1867, the houses mentioned in the agreement of 1850 were not standing; and that mentioned in the agreement of 1855 had been altered. The only explanation of that circumstance was what was understood by the Court to be a suggestion made at the hearing of the cause by the learned Counsel for the plaintiffs that the descriptions given in the agreements of 1850 and 1855 of the properties therein respectively comprised had been followed in the agreement of August, 1867, in order to secure their return by the defendant, on his giving up possession to the lessors, in the same state in which they were at the respective periods of the agreements of 1850 and 1855. In 1870, the bungalow or mission house which had been built on the site of one of those leased in 1850 to Messrs. Jackson and Welton, and which had been occupied as a residence by the defendant and other missionaries, was burnt down; and the existing mission house was built in its place on a site nearly corresponding to the site of that which had been burnt down. The new structure had an upper storey, which did not exist in the house which was burnt down; and the defendant said he had been told by some Mandarins that its height was offensive to their superstitions. The plaintiffs in their petition complained that the defendant had, without any proper license or authority, erected a wall which wrongfully en-

* Not in the original.

closed, together with a portion of the ground comprised in the agreement of August, 1867, other ground and several famous and memorial rocks standing thereon, wrongfully claimed by him under that agreement. It appeared that the wall now standing had been erected by the defendant in 1876 in place of another wall; and, upon the evidence, I find that it had then been thrown out at one corner of it about half a foot beyond the position of the original enclosing wall. The evidence for the plaintiffs showed that no part of the land on which the wall was erected was temple land; but the defendant contended that, except as to the encroachment just mentioned, it stood on land comprised in the agreement of August, 1867. But, whether this be so or not, the evidence for the plaintiffs showed that no part of the land on which the wall was erected was Temple land. The petition also stated that during the year 1878 the defendant, without any proper license or authority, proceeded to erect on ground enclosed within the wall just mentioned, a lofty and prominent structure of foreign design; that the gentry and inhabitants of Foochow complained to the local authorities and the matter was referred to the British Consul; that negotiations ensued and certain terms of arrangement which had been arrived at were referred to England for settlement; that pending such settlement the defendant wrongfully and in breach of good faith proceeded with the said building, and, when the same was nearly completed it was burnt by a mob; that the walls of the building were still standing, and that the defendant claimed to hold the land on which such building was erected under the agreement of August, 1867. The allegations just mentioned did not in any way affect the questions which the Court had to determine. The defendant by his answer denied some of the allegations of the petition; but the answer raised no material issue. It was stated in evidence that the land on which the Tao Shan Kwan stands is Government property and belongs to the Emperor, and that the temple was built by public subscription, and belongs to the public of the city of Foochow. It was also admitted at the bar by the learned Counsel for the plaintiffs that they had no estate in the temple; and it was said that they were merely directors of it. Several associations, thirteen in all, which existed in Foochow, were formed for the purpose of keeping the Tao Shan Kwan temple in repair and enabling its services to be conducted, and the associations subsisted solely for those purposes. Each association had, for the most part, its separate object in connection with the worship of the temple; but they all subscribed in common for its repairs. A person became a member of one of the associations by the payment of a subscription after election by the other members of the association. The associations were managed by directors chosen from the general body of their respective members; and the directors of the several associations were directors of the temple. The first consideration which arises in the determination of this case is the principle which is to govern the Court in interpreting the contract of August, 1867. Is it to be interpreted by the law of England, or by the law of China? The contract was executed in China; and it relates to land situate in China; and in conformity with the general principle applicable to cases involving the construction of contracts relating to land, which is that the law of the place where the land, the subject of the contract, is situate, governs its construction, the law of China applicable to the contract in question must govern its construction. The mode of procedure of the Court which is resorted to for the purpose of enforcing the contract is to be adopted, and the law to be applied in interpreting the contract must be given in evidence to the Court as a fact by professional or official witnesses, inasmuch as since their position requires sufficient knowledge to prove the law, it may be presumed that they possess it. (The Sussex Peerage, Case. 11 Clarke & Fin. 85; Duchess di Sora v. Phillips, 2 New R. 553; Taylor on Evid. § 1280 A 4th Edit.) The late Mr. Burge, in his commentaries on Colonial and Foreign Law (vol. 4, par. 2, ch. 12, p. 577), said—"It is admitted by all jurists that the transfer of and title to real property must be regulated by the *lex loci rei sitæ*." "The general principal of the common law is that the law of the place where real or immoveable property is situate exclusively governs in respect to the rights of the parties, the modes of transfer and the solemnities which should accompany them. The title, therefore, to real property can be acquired, passed, and lost only according to the *lex loci rei sitæ*." (Story's Conflict of Laws, sec. 424, 2nd edit.)—"The consent of the tribunals acting under the Common Law, both in England and America, is, in a practical sense, absolutely uniform on the same subject. All the authorities in both countries, so far as they go, recognise the principle in its fullest import, that real estate or immoveable property is exclusively subject to the laws of the government within whose territory it is situate." *Ibid*, sect. 428, "Contracts to be effectual must be in the form prescribed by the *lex loci*." *Ibid*, sect 435—The principle seems to be founded upon the inconvenience which it would be to any nation to suffer property, locally and permanently situate within its territory, to be subject to be transferred and dealt with by any other laws than its own; and thus introduce into the bosom of its own jurisprudence all the innumerable diversities of foreign laws to regulate its own titles to such property, many of which laws can be imperfectly ascertained, and many of which may become matters of subtle controversy (*Ibid*, sect. 440.) In the present case, two witnesses were called on behalf of the plaintiffs to prove the law applicable to the contract. One, Ting Kia Wai, being interpreted, described himself as follows:—"I am an officer at Peking in the service of the Emperor. I am Viceroy of Chihli. I have been Prefect in Foochow for three years, and I was previously in the Fokien province as an official over thirty years. I have held the office of District Magistrate as well as Prefect and Sub-prefect in the Fo-kien province. As District Magistrate and Prefect and Sub-Prefect, I had to administer justice in civil matters. . . . . I have had to decide questions arising on similar documents," that is, on documents similar to the agreement of August, 1867. The other witness called to prove the law of China applicable to the contract was Ching Che Yeo. Being interpreted, he said—"I am Hau Kwan District Magistrate and in the service of the Emperor of China. There are two District Magistrates in the city of Foochow, the Ming and the Hau Kwan. Part of my duties as District Magistrate consists in the administration of justice in civil matters and in putting the official seal to documents between Chinese and between foreigners and between foreigners and Chinese. I am acquainted with the laws and customs of this province (that is, the province of Fokien in which Foochow is situate), as regards leases. It is part of my duty to adjudicate on leases." When these witnesses were asked, the former what was the law of China, and the latter what was the law of the province of Fokien applicable to the agreement of August, 1867, Mr. Hannen, on behalf of the defendant, objected that, as foreign laws were not within the cognisance of this Court, and nothing had been stated in the petition with reference of the construction of that agreement being governed by the law of China, evidence was not admissible to prove what that law was. My opinion was that as the agreement had been stated in the petition, and it thereby appeared that it related to lands in China, and that as it was a well recognized principle of English law that the *lex loci rei sitæ*, or the law of the place where the property is situate, of which evidence must be given to the Court as a fact, was to be observed in the construction of agreements relating to land, the law of China with reference to the agreement need not be averred; and I accordingly overruled the objection. The witness, Ting Kia Wai, on being asked what is the law of China applicable to the agreement of August, 1867, said, "If rent is owing, the landlord can take back his house. If no rent is owing, the lessor cannot let to anyone else; but if the landlord wishes to have the house for himself the the tenant must give it up to the landlord. The landlord generally gives a month or two's notice. If the tenant has been in occupation for a long time, then it is at the option of the landlord either to charge rent for a month or two or to let the tenant occupy for a month or two rent free. Under an agreement of this kind a tenant would not be allowed to erect any buildings, nor would he be allowed to alter buildings already erected at the time of the agreement so as to alter their character." The same witness said that the words in the agreement which are translated "if the rent does not get into arrear the place may not be let to any one else," are what in England would be called in the legal profession "common form" in a lease for no definite period, and that "if a lease were in perpetuity it would be expressed to be in perpetuity;" and, in reply to Mr. Hannen, that witness said, "If a house is burnt down and the tenant rebuilds, an agreement is come to first by which it may be agreed how long the tenant may occupy before giving up possession to the landlord. There is no custom that tenant should rebuild after a house is burnt down without coming to an agreement with his landlord." The witness, Ching Che Yeo, when asked what is the law of the province of Fokien in regard to the instrument of August, 1867, said, "The instrument is a temporary lease, and not a perpetual one; and if the landlord wishes to have the property back and resume possession he can do so under this agreement." And when asked whether under the words "rent to be paid quarterly in advance," it is at the option of the landlord to refuse rent or not, he replied, —"If the landlord refuses rent, the tenant has to go at once according to law. Generally a tenant has about half a month to find a house. Whether rent is to be paid for that period is at the option of the landlord. If the parties went to a magistrate, he would say the tenant should go at once. If the rent were paid three months in advance, the tenant then would have to go at end of three months, if the landlord refused rent. The landlord might give the tenant ten days or a month, or a month and-a-half, according as he chose, before taking possession. Under the words in the agreement, 'the landlord cannot let to any one else than the tenant,' if the landlord wanted the premises for himself he could have them back." By the agreement of August, 1867, it was provided that the rent should be paid quarterly in advance to the Trade Committee. Since June, 1878, the directors of the Tao Shau Kwan had refused, through the Board of Trade, to receive the rent reserved by the agreement of August, 1867; but Mr. Consul Sinclair stated that he was not quite certain whether he had communicated that refusal to the defendant. No evidence was given on the part of the defendant as to the law of China applicable to the agreement of August, 1867. Each of the witnesses, Ting Kia Wai and Ching Che Yeo, the former speaking of the law of China and the latter of the law of the province of Fokien, said that if the landlord wanted the land for himself he could resume possession. Neither of those witnesses was either asked or expressed any opinion as to the right of the landlord to take back the premises if he did not himself require them. The conclusion at which I arrive on their evidence is that the landlord, in order to establish the right to the resumption of property leased in such terms as those mentioned in the agreement of August, 1867, would have to show that he *bonâ fide* required the property for himself, or, in the present case, for the purposes of the temple. But there is no averment in the petition, nor is there any proof of such fact. The absence of any evidence that the plaintiffs required the property compised in the agreement of August, 1867, either for themselves or for the purposes of the Tao Shan Kwan, seems to me to prevent the Court from making a decree declaratory of the plaintiffs' present right to resume possession of that property. If the plaintiffs relied upon the law of China in support of their right under the agreement of August, 1867, to take back the property therein comprised, they ought at all events to have shown by evidence that they required such property for the purposes of the Tao Shan Kwan Temple. That they have not done. No point was taken at the bar in avoidance to this extent of the agreement of August, 1867, that two, at all events, of the houses therein described were not then standing. Nor was there any evidence to show that the agreement of August, 1867, was void on any other ground according to the law of China. Also, no evidence was given on the part of the plaintiffs as to the person or persons (if any) on whom Wolfe's interest in the agreement of August, 1867, would devolve in case of his death, before the property therein comprised was required for the purposes of the temple or he had given up possession of it. The petition prayed that it might be ordered and decreed that the defendant had by his unauthorized and wrongful dealings with the land and buildings comprised in the agreement of August, 1867, forfeited all his right and title in and to such lands and buildings. No evidence was given on the plaintiffs' part to show that the defendant had so dealt with the property comprised in the agreement of August, 1867, as to entitle the plaintiffs to the relief here prayed. The rebuilding of the Mission House in its present form after the former one had been burnt down in 1870, was not shown to be an act of forfeiture on the part of the defendant according to the law of China. The removal, too, of the houses comprised in the agreement of 1850, and the building of other structures of a different character in their place had occurred prior to August, 1867. The petition also prayed that the boundaries of the land comprised in the agreement of August, 1867, might be ascertained and declared. No declaration that the court could make under the head of relief here asked would be conclusive and binding on the rights of the adjoining land owners, they not being before the court. Such a declaration in this suit might give rise to greater difficulties than it was intended to obviate. With reference to the land let verbally to the Missionary, George Smith, in 1855, the evidence, in my view, shows that the land on which the college stood which was burnt down in August, 1878, was a part of that land. Upon the hearing of the cause, authorities in the English courts of law were cited, and it may be asked what would be the opinion of the court on the agreement of August, 1867, if it had to decide on the validity or invalidity of that agreement by reference to English law exclusively, and not with any reference to Chinese law. If I am right in the view I have expressed, that the case is governed by Chinese law, any expression of opinion of mine on the head now suggested would be of little avail, and perhaps out of place. I may here observe that the case itself is an anomalous one, and not likely to be of value as a precedent. Nor is the value of the interests involved in it of much moment. But other circumstances have drawn to it a factitious degree of attention which neither the value of the interests involved nor the importance of the points raised justify. The order made by the court is as follows: Dismiss the petition so far as the same relates to the agreement of September, 1866, as against the defendant John Richard Wolfe, and as against him as being sued on behalf of the English Church Missionary Society, with costs to be paid by the plaintiffs to the defendant and to the English Church Missionary Society in the same manner as if the petition had, as soon as it was amended, been demurred to so far as it related to the said agreement of September, 1866, and such demurrer had been allowed. Declare that the agreement of August, 1867, is a valid and subsisting agreement, and that the same ought to be carried into effect. Declare that the said agreement of August, 1867, has been in no way forfeited. Declare that the plaintiffs will be entitled to resume possession of the property in the occupation of the defendant as lessee of the plaintiffs under the said agreement of August, 1867, on their *bonâ fide* requiring the same for the purposes of the Tao

Shau Kwan Temple, and giving three calendar months' notice thereof to the defendant; such notice to expire on one of the quarterly days on which rent is payable under the said agreement of August, 1867.

Declare that the defendant is entitled to hold, for the term of his natural life, the property comprised in the agreement of August, 1867, subject to the payment of the rent thereby reserved, quarterly in advance, and subject also to the plaintiffs' right to resume possession of the same property as before declared. No further costs on either side.

(Signed) GEORGE FRENCH,
Chief Justice.

Spotted something that isn't quite right?

Let us know and we'll fix it for future reprints. And as a thank you for your diligence, we'll send you a free Sothis book of your choice.

publisher@sothis.press

This page intentionally left blank

Made in the USA
Monee, IL
08 November 2026

68106066R00059